"Dr. Thoennes is a masterful teache   ıder-
standing, he comes to grips with the   ;pel.
The beauty of following Christ coı   ader
will want to fall in love with Jesus a

   Robert E. Coleman, Distinguisł   .ism,
Gordon-Conwell Theological Seminary; author, *The Master Plan of Evangelism*

"Socrates's well-known statement, 'The unexamined life is not worth living,' is an entirely appropriate start to *Life's Biggest Questions*. Stepping outside of one's day-to-day existence to reflect on the big-picture questions is understandable and commendable. This book clearly, concisely, and thoughtfully presents answers from an evangelical Christian perspective. Thoennes is not only able to articulate Christian theology and history, but also help readers think through the implications for their own lives."

      Heather Campbell, Vice President, Atheist Coalition of San Diego

"Helpful, concise, accessible: this book will provide clarity and conviction for those looking for answers to the big questions."

      Josh Moody, Senior Pastor, College Church in Wheaton

"In clear, insightful, and relevant ways Thoennes tackles some of life's most bewildering questions. His treatment of the perennial dilemmas that have plagued inquisitive minds avoids easy clichés and unrealistic answers. Thoennes artfully and biblically turns the question marks of sincere seekers into exclamation points that undergird life with confidence and certainty. This book is a one-of-a-kind resource among similar books that are either too light and unrealistic or too heavy to get our heads around. As such, it is a welcome arrival and an important read—the kind of book that you are happy to share with a friend!"

      Joe Stowell, President, Cornerstone University

"A concise and engaging introduction to the core beliefs of the Christian faith that would be helpful both to followers of Christ and those who are investigating the Christian faith and want to understand what Christians believe. Not only does Thoennes show how these beliefs are rooted in Scripture but he also helps us see how they practically relate to the Christian life."

      Keith Johnson, Director, Theological Education and Development,
                                  Campus Crusade for Christ

"A thorough and accessible introduction to what Christians believe and why we believe it. Thoennes encourages believers and nonbelievers alike to examine their assumptions in light of biblical truth and to consider the life-altering implications of their beliefs. *Life's Biggest Questions* is an encouraging, pastoral introduction to Christianity. Thoennes makes the case that all Christians—from the seminary student to the homemaker—will benefit from the study of theology, and that our lives are profoundly affected by a true knowledge of God. Reading this book has been an encouragement to my faith—bolstering and clarifying my understanding of truth and deepening my appreciation of God and his beautiful work of redemption. The discussion questions at the end of each chapter illustrate the practical significance of theology and will lead readers to fruitful examination of their beliefs and helpful applications of doctrinal truths. Small groups, churches, and individuals will benefit from Thoennes's pastoral invitation to engage with the most important questions in life."

Laura Rosenkranz, homemaker; educator

"It is refreshing to see a book that addresses our deepest concerns from a distinctively theological perspective. Professor Thoennes is a master communicator, and *Life's Biggest Questions* is marked by an accessible, interesting style. The book is filled with content and distinctively characterized by repeated examples of practical application. It is a fun read and would make an excellent text for a course in theology or Christian worldview."

J. P. Moreland, Distinguished Professor of Philosophy, Talbot School of Theology; author, *The God Question*

"This splendid book provides clear and concise answers to life's greatest questions. It is a perfect volume for intelligent truth seekers and Christians who want to build a firmer biblical foundation for their faith."

Lyle Dorsett, Billy Graham Professor of Evangelism, Beeson Divinity School, Samford University; author, *A Passion for Souls: The Life of D. L. Moody*

"People without questions may have deluded themselves into thinking they have all the answers. Being finite and fallen should awaken curiosity in the heart of any honest person. Thoennes does more than encourage the asking of questions. He directs readers to the Scriptures as a source of answers both wise and good. Furthermore, he cultivates curiosities to morph into questions that ripen into the rich fruit of wonder, awe, and eventually worship. I know this, because he is my friend. My life has been encouraged by his personal counsel as well as by this book."

Jerry Root, Associate Professor of Evangelism and Leadership, Wheaton College; coauthor, *The Sacrament of Evangelism*

"This is an easy read about profound truths. Thoennes's book is bigger on the inside than it appears on the outside. He writes with elegant simplicity about biblical doctrine, with clear conceptualization and user-friendly prose concerning the basic doctrines of the Scriptures. Thoennes's trustworthy, sturdy, and receptor-oriented writing puts the nourishment of the Word within the reader's reach. It is a joy to think after him. Since our spirituality and relationship with God flows directly from our theology and our beliefs about God, Thoennes's work will be of interest to anyone looking for a basic biblical foundation for soulcare and spiritual formation work."

Betsy A. Barber, Director, Center for Spiritual Renewal, Biola University; Associate Director, Institute for Spiritual Formation, Talbot School of Theology

LIFE'S BIGGEST
QUESTIONS

LIFE'S BIGGEST
QUESTIONS

WHAT THE BIBLE SAYS ABOUT
THE THINGS THAT MATTER MOST

ERIK THOENNES

CROSSWAY

WHEATON, ILLINOIS

Life's Biggest Questions: What the Bible Says about the Things That Matter Most
Copyright © 2011 by Crossway
Published by Crossway
   1300 Crescent Street
   Wheaton, Illinois 60187

The text and charts in this book are adapted from the *ESV Study Bible*.

Interior design and typesetting: Lakeside Design Plus
Cover design: Studio Gearbox
First printing 2011
Printed in the United States of America

Trade Paperback ISBN: 978-1-4335-2671-8
PDF ISBN: 978-1-4335-2672-5
Mobipocket ISBN: 978-1-4335-2673-2
ePub ISBN: 978-1-4335-2674-9

Library of Congress Cataloging-in-Publication Data
Thoennes, Erik.
 Life's biggest questions : what the Bible says about the things that matter most
/ Erik Thoennes.
   p. cm.
 Includes bibliographical references and index.
 ISBN 978-1-4335-2671-8 (tp)
   1. Bible—Examinations, questions, etc. 2. Theology, Doctrinal—Miscellanea.
I. Title.
BS612.T465 2011
230—dc22

                     2011001942

Crossway is a publishing ministry of Good News Publishers.

VP	23	22	21	20	19	18	17	16	15	14	13	12	11
14	13	12	11	10	9	8	7	6	5	4	3	2	

To my delightful wife, Donna, my precious daughters, Caroline and Paige, the faithful saints at Grace Evangelical Free Church of La Mirada, and my earnest students at Biola University.

By God's grace,
your lives have helped me to better understand
and believe his answers to life's biggest questions.

CONTENTS

LIST OF FIGURES

ACKNOWLEDGMENTS

I would like to thank the following people for the contributions they have made to make this book possible: My faithful, beautiful wife, Donna, whose wisdom, care, insight, discernment, grace, sense of humor, and patience have been a reservoir of joy since we first met in high school; my parents and Jean Parett who faithfully pray for me; the elders and shepherds at Grace Evangelical Free Church of La Mirada, with whom it has been my joy to serve our flock under the authority of the Great Shepherd; Wayne Grudem, J. Julius Scott, Steven Roy, and Robert Coleman, who have helped to shape my thinking and teaching greatly; Barry Corey, Dennis Dirks, Michael Wilkins, David Talley, and the rest of the godly faculty and staff at Talbot School of Theology/ Biola University, with whom it is a privilege to serve our Savior together; Lane Dennis, Justin Taylor, and the other good people at Crossway, who honor Christ and edify the church with their excellent work. My deepest gratitude goes to our heavenly Father, who has answered our deepest questions by sending his Son, so that through the power of the Spirit we can be set free from sin and death.

WHAT ARE LIFE'S BIGGEST QUESTIONS?

"The unexamined life is not worth living." —Socrates

Everyone wants a meaningful life. There is nothing more human than wondering what that means. Even in days filled with shallowness and countless distractions, when the light goes out at the end of the day and you lie in bed staring at the ceiling, you aren't human if you don't think about what it all means. But a meaningful life can be found only by asking good, honest questions. Good questions get to the foundational things that everyone wonders about. Humans in every generation and culture have always asked questions such as, is there a God? What is a human being? Is there such a thing as sin and, if so, can anything be done about it? Is there life after death? Even if you try to ignore questions like these, all it takes is an inquisitive child or the death of a loved one to bring life's big questions back to the surface. Asking questions assumes there are answers and that they can be found. But many today wonder if objective truth may be found, or if all we have are personal and cultural conventions. Even if absolute truth does exist, can we break out of our limited perspectives and discover it? Many increasingly think we are all left to ourselves to make truth up as we go and there is no way to know what is true or false, right or wrong, good or bad, worthwhile or empty. The Roman governor Pontius Pilate seemed to foreshadow our growing contemporary cynicism about truth when he asked Jesus, "What is truth?" before handing him over to be unjustly murdered (John 18:38).

Into this mounting confusion, uncertainty, and despair, Jesus Christ breaks in, declaring that he is "the way, and the truth, and the life . . ." (John 14:6) and that he alone can bring life that is abundantly fulfilling and eternally significant (John 10:10). He is the one who restores peace with God and brings the answers we long to know. He not only provides the answers we long for, he *is* the answer. The Bible is the primary source for knowing Jesus and the answers he taught. While many acknowledge the wisdom and goodness of Jesus, it is also vital to realize that he viewed the Scriptures as God's Word and the foundation for answering life's greatest questions. This book is an effort to clearly and concisely present those answers. If you aren't really sure what Christians actually believe or if you've been a Christian for a long time but want to solidify the foundation of your faith, I hope this short book can accomplish both of those goals.

GETTING TO THE POINT

This paragraph gets to the bottom line of what Christians believe. The Bible is inspired by God and is centrally about God and what it means to have a relationship with him. God has always existed as one God in three persons, Father, Son, and Holy Spirit. He has always been revealing himself and communicating everything we will ever need to know to live profoundly meaningful lives. The basic story line of the Bible reveals a loving and holy God who created everything just as he wanted it to be as an expression of his excellence and beauty, and he declared everything *very* good. At the pinnacle of his creation God made humans in his image, which means they are more like him than anything else. Human purpose is found fundamentally in relationship with our Creator, depending on him for everything, honoring him, and seeing all of life as an act of worship of him. "Worthy are you, our Lord and God, to receive glory and honor and power, for you created all things, and by your will they existed and were created" (Rev. 4:11). Tragically, since Adam and Eve's fall, all humans are born in rebellion against God (Rom. 3:10–12). God rightly judges this sin, and we incur his wrath and sin's penalty, which is death (Heb. 9:27). God loves mankind so much that he will not let us settle for anything less than satisfaction in him as our greatest joy. He provides a way of escape from this judgment by sending the eternal Son of God to become a man so that he can represent us in his perfect life, sacrificial death, and victorious resurrection. Christ unites divine and human in himself so that he can become the only mediator between a holy God and rebellious humans. "For Christ also suffered once for sins, the righteous for the unrighteous, that he might bring us to God, being put to death in the flesh but made alive in the spirit" (1 Pet. 3:18). The forgiveness humanity so desperately needs but is unable to accomplish is achieved by God himself through the person and work of Christ. When the Holy Spirit uses the Word of God primarily through the witness of his church to reveal God's awesome character, sinners see their need for a Savior and repent and trust Christ for forgiveness and a restored relationship with God as Father. All the obedience and righteousness of Christ becomes theirs through their adoption into God's family. Holy Spirit–enabled conversion leads to Holy Spirit–empowered growth in

3. What kind of authority do you think the Bible deserves to have in your life? What authoritative influence has it had in your life? Why do (or don't) you allow it to have authoritative weight in your life?

4. What has been your impression of the Christian faith before now? What has influenced you to come to this impression? What do you hope this book will help you with the most?

For Further Study

The brief summaries of the doctrines of the Christian faith found in this book are good starting points for deeper study and reflection. To that end, recommendations of key resources for further study are provided here and at the end of each chapter.

Craig, William Lane. *Reasonable Faith: Christian Truth and Apologetics*. Wheaton, IL: Crossway, 2008.

Craig, William Lane, and Chad Meister, eds. *God Is Great, God Is Good: Why Believing in God Is Reasonable and Responsible*. Downers Grove, IL: InterVarsity Press, 2009.

Keller, Timothy. *The Reason for God: Belief in an Age of Skepticism*. New York: Riverhead, 2008.

Lewis, C. S. *Mere Christianity*. San Francisco: Harper, 1952.

Moreland, J. P. *Love Your God with All Your Mind: The Role of Reason in the Life of the Soul*. Colorado Springs: NavPress, 1997.

———. *Scaling the Secular City: A Defense of Christianity*. Grand Rapids, MI: Baker, 1987.

Sproul, R. C. *The Consequences of Ideas: Understanding the Concepts That Shaped Our World*. Wheaton, IL: Crossway, 2009.

Wells, David. *No Place for Truth, or, Whatever Happened to Evangelical Theology?* Grand Rapids, MI: Eerdmans, 1993.

DOES GOD EXIST?

"The worst moment for the atheist is when he is really thankful and has nobody to thank."
—Dante Gabriel Rossetti

The question of God's existence seems like a logical place to start to answer life's biggest questions. So, you might think that the Bible starts here and makes it a major priority to argue for God's existence, but it doesn't. Rather, it assumes God's existence from the first verse to the last. It also assumes that God has revealed himself in such obvious ways in creation and human experience (Rom. 1:19–21) that to deny his existence would be foolish (Ps. 14:1). The Bible tells us that because of God's personal nature, he must reveal himself if we are to know him personally. God has revealed himself to us in two ways: through special revelation and general revelation.

SPECIAL REVELATION

The Bible is God's written revelation of who he is and what he has done in redemptive history. Humans need this divine, transcendent perspective in order to break out of their subjective, culturally bound, fallen limitations. Through God's written Word, we may overcome error, grow in sanctification, minister effectively to others, and enjoy abundant lives as God intends.

GENERAL REVELATION

General revelation is given by God to all people at all times. This revelation is found both in the external creation (Ps. 19:1: "The heavens declare the glory of God . . .") and in internal human experience (Rom. 1:19–20: "What can be known about God is plain to them, because God has shown it to them. For his invisible attributes, namely, his eternal power and divine nature, have been clearly perceived, ever since the creation of the world, in the things that have been made. So they are without excuse"). General revelation shows several of God's attributes, such as his existence, power, creativity, and wisdom; in addition, the testimony of human conscience also provides some evidence of God's moral standards to all human beings (Rom. 2:14–15). Therefore, from general revelation all people have *some* knowledge that God exists, *some* knowledge of his character, and *some* knowledge of his moral standards. This results in an awareness of guilt before God, as people instinctively know that they have not lived up to his moral requirements. Thus, in the many false religions that have been invented, people attempt to assuage their sense of guilt.

But general revelation does not disclose the only true solution to man's guilt before God: the forgiveness of sins that comes through Jesus Christ. This means that general revelation does not provide personal knowledge of God as a loving Father who redeems his people and establishes a covenant with them. For this, one needs special revelation, which God has provided in his historical supernatural activities, in the Bible, and definitively in Jesus Christ.

ARGUMENTS FOR THE EXISTENCE OF GOD

Arguments from External General Revelation

The Cosmological Argument. The cosmological (*cosmos* = world) argument starts from the *existence* of the world and argues for an *ultimate cause* (i.e., a Creator). The existence of anything requires a sufficient cause for its existence. This is a basic assumption of science itself, and there is nothing in all creation that does not follow this principle. The world itself must have a sufficient cause because it gives absolutely no indication of being either eternal or self-created. Basic presuppositions of science and logic go against either an eternal or self-generated world. This leaves us with the need for a sufficient cause that is eternal, self-existent, and outside of creation to explain the world's existence. The Bible teaches that God miraculously created the world out of nothing, which is the most plausible explanation for how we ended up with the world as we know it.

The Teleological Argument. The teleological (*telos* = goal) argument starts from the *nature* of the world and argues for the nature of the *Creator* (i.e., a Designer). It starts with the creation and argues not just for a creator, but for a creator who is intelligent, personal, wise, purposeful, and powerful. This argument moves from the need for a cause of the world to the need to explain its amazing intelligent design. The world not only acts caused, it acts intelligently caused. There is regularity and order in the cosmos that demands a wise, intelligent creator behind it. As Voltaire said, "If a watch proves the existence of a watchmaker but the universe does not prove the existence of a great architect, then I consent to be called a fool." How can one ponder the solar system, DNA, the brain, an eye, or a flower and not say with the psalmist, "The heavens declare the glory of God . . ." (Ps. 19:1); and, "I praise you, for I am fearfully and wonderfully made . . ." (Ps. 139:14)?

Arguments from Internal General Revelation

The Argument from Personality. It's easy to recognize the radical difference between personal beings and impersonal things. Personal beings laugh, think, feel, decide, and reflect, and they are self-conscious. If there is no personal being who created the world, how do you explain the existence of persons? How could an impersonal, random process ever produce complex personal beings? Can the personal ever come from the impersonal? It seems obvious that no matter how much time or chance it's given, an impersonal process can never produce something personal. Therefore there must be a personal Creator responsible for humanity.

The Argument from Beauty. The understanding and appreciation of beauty is a universal human experience. Although there can be wide disagreement about what is and isn't beautiful, the understanding of beauty and the ability to enjoy it is common to all human cultures. How can you explain this universal aesthetic appreciation, apart from a divine artist who not only created beautiful things, but also created humans with the capacity to admire them? Natural selection or naturalistic explanations cannot account for art museums.

The Argument from Morality. All human beings have a deep inner sense of right and wrong. This "Law of Human Nature" has amazing similarities across cultures. Even those who claim to believe that morality is relative and socially constructed know intuitively that rape, or racism, or genocide are immoral, regardless of anyone's opinion to the contrary. Even though this moral sense gets suppressed and ignored, moral outrage and admiration for goodness are a constant assumption throughout human history. How can we account for this apart from a divine judge who created us and instills a sense of morality in humans?

The Argument from Meaning. All humans want to know that their lives matters. We all have a deep longing for significance and meaning that transcends mere animalistic gratification. Where does this universal human desire come from apart from a God who created us to have meaningful lives and instilled this yearning in our hearts? As C. S. Lewis said, "If I find in myself a desire which no experience in this world can satisfy, the most probable explanation is that I was made for another world."[1]

The Argument from Religious Experience. Humans have been described as being incurably religious. Throughout history, humans have invariably had a sense of something bigger and beyond us to whom we owe our existence and worship. While there have been significant differences in how God has been conceived, there has nonetheless been a deeply religious bent to human experience. In spite of modern theories of the inevitable secularization of the Western world, these predictions have proven thoroughly untrue. While atheism may seem like it is on the rise today, it is important to realize that atheism is mostly the invention of a small number of modern, white, Western, urban males who seem to have lost a sense of their dependence and frailty before God. Even efforts to explain away the religious instinct, such as Marxism and Freudian psychology, end up replacing God with views of realty that sound very "religious." How are we to explain this religious instinct apart from a God who created us for relationship with him and a longing for that relationship? As Augustine pointed out, we are restless until we find our rest in the God who made us for himself.

EVALUATION

These arguments do not "prove" God's existence because he isn't a math equation or something you can put under a micro-

---

[1]C. S. Lewis, *Mere Christianity* (1952; New York: Touchstone, 1996), 121.

scope or discover through unaided reason and experience alone. These arguments present a cumulative case to doubt atheism and consider the claims of the Bible. When taken together, they give good reasons to believe that reality as we know it is the creation of a powerful, wise, personal Creator. The arguments do not, however, convince us of a God who loves us and is willing to forgive our sins and call us his children. They don't give us an understanding of God who revealed himself in Christ and will right all the wrong in the world. For that, we need to seek him in his Word, where he has revealed himself most clearly, personally, and powerfully.

SCRIPTURE MEMORY AND MEDITATION

"The heavens declare the glory of God, and the sky above proclaims his handiwork." (Ps. 19:1)

Questions for Application and Discussion

1. When you have a deep sense of gratitude for something no human gave you (e.g., a sunset, health, life, mountains) do you feel inclined to worship? If so, where do you think that desire comes from?

2. The Bible says that the heavens declare the glory of God. What could help you to recognize that glory in nature?

3. As you read through the arguments in this chapter, were any of your doubts about God diminished? Are you better able to reasonably refute atheism?

4. Among the arguments discussed in this chapter, which ones did you find most helpful or convincing? Are your doubts about God mostly intellectual, moral, or experiential?

5. How might someone find meaning or morality apart from God?

For Further Study

Craig, William Lane. *Reasonable Faith: Christian Truth and Apologetics*. 3rd ed. Wheaton, IL: Crossway, 2008.

Frame, John M. *Apologetics to the Glory of God: An Introduction*. Phillipsburg, NJ: P&R, 1994.

France, R. T. *The Living God*. Downers Grove, IL: InterVarsity Press, 1970.

Geisler, Norman. *Christian Apologetics*. Grand Rapids, MI: Baker, 1976.

McDowell, Josh. *Evidence That Demands a Verdict*. San Bernardino, CA: Here's Life, 1972, 1979.

Moreland, J. P., and Kai Nielsen. *Does God Exist? The Debate between Theists & Atheists*. Amherst, NY: Prometheus, 1993.

_____. *Scaling the Secular City: A Defense of Christianity*. Grand Rapids, MI: Baker, 1987.

Swinburne, Richard. *The Existence of God*. 2nd ed. New York: Oxford University Press, 2004.

3

WHAT DOES IT MEAN TO KNOW AND LOVE GOD?

"The most important thing about a man is what comes into his mind when he thinks about God." —A. W. Tozer

The study of theology is considered by many to be dry, boring, irrelevant, and complicated. But for those who want to know God, the study of theology is indispensable. The word *theology* comes from two Greek words, *theos* ("God") and *logos* ("word"). The study of theology is an effort to make definitive statements about God in an accurate, coherent, relevant way, based on God's self-revelation. Doctrine equips people to fulfill their primary purpose, which is to glorify and delight in God through a deep personal knowledge of him. Meaningful relationship with God depends on correct knowledge of him.

Any theological system that distinguishes between "rational propositions about God" and "a personal relationship with God" fails to see the necessary connection between love and knowledge. The capacity to love, enjoy, and tell others about a person is increased by greater knowledge of that person. Love and knowledge go hand in hand. Good lovers are students of the beloved. Knowledge and love of God is the goal of theology.

Knowledge without devotion is cold, dead orthodoxy. Devotion without knowledge is irrational instability. But true knowledge of God seeks to understand everything from his perspective. Theology is learning to think God's thoughts after him. It is to learn what God loves and hates, and to see, hear, think, and act the way he does. Knowing how God thinks is the first step in becoming godly.

Many like to think that just being a "good" person and "loving" God, without emphasizing doctrine, is preferable. But being a good person can mean radically different things depending on what someone thinks "good" is, or what constitutes a "person." Loving God will look very different depending on one's conception of "God" or "love." The fundamental connections between belief and behavior, and between love and knowledge, demand a rigorous pursuit of truth for those wanting to love God and to be godly. Hebrews 5:11–6:3 teaches that deepening theological understanding equips one to be able to differentiate good from evil, and it exhorts believers to mature in their knowledge of God and his ways:

> For though by this time you ought to be teachers, you need someone to teach you again the basic principles of the oracles of God. You need milk, not solid food, for everyone who lives on milk is unskilled in the word of righteousness, since he is a child. But solid food is for the mature, for those who have their powers of discernment trained by constant practice to distinguish good from evil. Therefore let us leave the elementary doctrine of Christ and go on to maturity. . . . (Heb. 5:12–6:1)

Christian theology is based on the belief that God exists, is personal, can be known, and has revealed himself. These presuppositions motivate theologians to devote themselves to a passionate pursuit of knowledge from God's Word. Unfortunately, the word "theologian" is used almost exclusively for vocational theologians rather than for anyone earnestly devoted to knowing God. On one level everyone who thinks about God is a theologian. But a believer whose life is consumed with knowing his Lord is most certainly a theologian, and theologians are committed to truth.

Loving God means loving truth. God is a God of truth; he *is* truth. In Scripture, all three persons of the Trinity are vitally related to truth (see fig. 3.1).

Figure 3.1

TRUTH AND THE TRINITY

Father	"So that he who blesses himself in the land shall bless himself by the God of truth, and he who takes an oath in the land shall swear by the God of truth because the former troubles are forgotten and are hidden from my eyes" (Isa. 65:16).
	"What if some were unfaithful? Does their faithlessness nullify the faithfulness of God? By no means! Let God be true though every one were a liar, as it is written, 'That you may be justified in your words, and prevail when you are judged'" (Rom. 3:3–4).
Son	"Jesus said to him, 'I am the way, and the truth, and the life. No one comes to the Father except through me'" (John 14:6).
	"But that is not the way you learned Christ!—assuming that you have heard about him and were taught in him, as the truth is in Jesus" (Eph. 4:20–21).
Spirit	"But when the Helper comes, whom I will send to you from the Father, the Spirit of truth, who proceeds from the Father, he will bear witness about me" (John 15:26).
	"When the Spirit of truth comes, he will guide you into all the truth, for he will not speak on his own authority, but whatever he hears he will speak, and he will declare to you the things that are to come" (John 16:13).

In light of this relationship between God and truth, it should be no surprise that the Great Commandment includes loving God with one's mind: "And you shall love the Lord your God with all your heart and with all your soul and with all your mind and with all your strength" (Mark 12:30, quoting Deut. 30:6). Fully loving God and obeying this Great Commandment requires actively engaging the mind in the pursuit of truth.

The second half of the Great Commandment—love your neighbor as yourself (Mark 12:31)—also requires a great commitment to truth. Love, kindness, and compassion must include profound concern that people understand the truth, since their lives depend on it. God meets our greatest need of relationship with him through an understanding of truth: "Of his own will [God] brought us forth *by the word of truth*, that we should be a kind of firstfruits of his creatures" (James 1:18; see 1 Pet. 1:23). Sanctification also happens by means of the truth: "Sanctify them in the truth; your word is truth" (John 17:17; see Rom. 12:2). Authentic discipleship is marked by knowing and obeying truth: "If you abide in my word, you are truly my disciples, and you will know the truth, and the truth will set you free" (John 8:31–32). Therefore, loving others involves having a deep desire that they understand truth. This is the reason the Great Commission has a vital teaching element. Making disciples of Christ involves teaching them to observe all he has commanded (Matt. 28:20). Jesus wants people to understand and obey truth and thereby find life in him. Failure to care whether loved ones understand the truth is failure to care about their abundant and eternal lives. People are judged and go to hell because they fail to love and obey God's truth (2 Thess. 2:11–13; see Rom. 1:18, 21, 25; James 1:18; 1 Pet. 1:23).

THEOLOGICAL METHOD

Systematic theology seeks to summarize biblical teaching on particular topics in order to draw definitive conclusions that intersect with life. God has revealed himself generally in nature and personally in human history. He has not only revealed himself in facts and statements, but what is objectively true of him has also been revealed in the subjective experience of people to whom he has revealed himself. God's revelation of himself recorded in the Bible is the foundation for knowing God today.

God's revelation in Scripture is rich, personal, and wedded to real life. But it can also be more difficult to understand than mere facts and propositions, because the historical context of the revelation is often foreign to modern people. Because revelation of God is personal and historical, the biblical understanding of God is progressive and cumulative. The theologian therefore must consider the historical context and progressive nature of revelation at every stage. The theological process must include careful study of biblical passages that are relevant to the question being answered. Furthermore, study of the Bible should be done with great sensitivity to the historical context of the passages being studied. This theological method has produced several focused areas of study.

THE THEOLOGICAL PROCESS

The theological process can be categorized under several aspects and disciplines (see fig. 3.2). In particular, systematic theology builds on the conclusions of exegesis and biblical theology. It attempts to summarize the teaching of Scripture in a brief, understandable, and carefully formulated statement. It involves appropriately *collecting*, *synthesizing*, and *understanding* all the relevant passages in the Bible on various topics, and then *summarizing* their teachings clearly so that we can know what to believe and how to live as God intends.

Figure 3.2

THE THEOLOGICAL PROCESS

Exegesis	The process of seeking to determine the correct meaning of a particular passage of Scripture.
Biblical theology	The study of scriptural revelation based on the historical framework presented in the Bible.
Systematic theology	A study that answers the question, "What does the whole Bible teach us today about a given topic?"
Historical theology	The study of how believers in different eras of the history of the church have understood various theological topics.
Philosophical theology	The study of theological topics primarily through the use of the tools and methods of philosophical reasoning and information gained from nature and reason ("general revelation") apart from the Bible.
Practical theology	The study of how to best apply theological truths to the life of the church and the world (including preaching, Christian education, counseling, evangelism, missions, church administration, worship, etc.).
Apologetics	The study of theology for the purpose of defending Christian teaching against criticism and distortion, and giving evidences of its credibility.

Reference to this sort of whole-Bible theology can be seen in Paul's insistence that he did not shrink back from declaring "the whole counsel of God" (Acts 20:27) and in Jesus's Great Commission that the church should "make disciples of all nations" by "teaching them to observe all that I have commanded you . . ." (Matt. 28:19–20). Jesus also uses this way of understanding the Bible as he takes his disciples through the Old Testament, showing how he is found throughout (Luke 24:27, 44).

MAJOR CATEGORIES OF STUDY IN SYSTEMATIC THEOLOGY

The major topics covered in the study of systematic theology can be seen in figure 3.3.

Fig. 3.3

STUDIES IN SYSTEMATIC THEOLOGY

Area of Study	Technical Title
Method and foundation	Prolegomena
The Bible	Bibliology
God	Theology proper
Humanity (or man)	Anthropology
Sin	Hamartiology
Christ	Christology
Holy Spirit	Pneumatology
Salvation	Soteriology
Church	Ecclesiology
Last things	Eschatology

ESSENTIAL VS. PERIPHERAL DOCTRINE

The ability to discern the relative importance of theological beliefs is vital for effective Christian life and ministry. Both the purity and unity of the church are at stake in this matter. The relative importance of theological issues can fall within four categories: (1) *absolutes* define the core beliefs of the Christian faith; (2) *convictions*, while not core beliefs, may have significant impact on the health and effectiveness of the church; (3) *opinions* are views or personal judgments that generally are not worth dividing over; and (4) *questions* are currently unsettled issues. These categories can be best visualized as concentric circles, similar to those on a dart board, with the absolutes as the "bull's-eye" (see fig. 3.4).

Into which category an issue falls should be determined by the cumulative force of at least eight considerations: (1) biblical clarity; (2) relevance to the character of God; (3) relevance to the essence of the gospel; (4) biblical frequency and significance (how often in Scripture it is taught, and what weight Scripture

Figure 3.4

DISCERNING THE WEIGHT OF BELIEFS

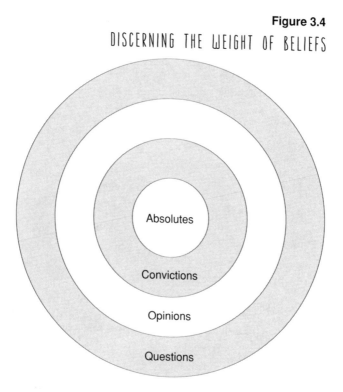

Absolutes

Convictions

Opinions

Questions

places upon it); (5) effect on other doctrines; (6) consensus among Christians (past and present); (7) effect on personal and church life; and (8) current cultural pressure to deny a teaching of Scripture. We should consider the cumulative weight of these criteria when determining the relative importance of particular beliefs. For instance, just the fact that a doctrine may go against the general consensus among believers (see item 6) does not necessarily mean it is wrong, although that might add some weight to the argument against it. All the categories should be considered collectively in determining how important an issue is to the Christian faith. The ability to rightly discern the difference between core doctrines and legitimately disputable matters will keep the church from either compromising important truth or needlessly dividing over peripheral issues.

SCRIPTURE MEMORY AND MEDITATION

"And you shall love the Lord your God with all your heart and with all your soul and with all your mind and with all your strength." (Mark 12:30)

Questions for Application and Discussion

1. What has been your attitude toward the study of doctrine? Has anything in this chapter helped to increase your appreciation of doctrine?

2. Can you think of any issues in your life that will improve with a better understanding of a particular doctrine?

3. How should a true understanding of God as the sovereign, wise Creator shape your daily life?

4. What are things you do (or should do) that demonstrate your conviction that truth really matters?

5. What are issues you would consider absolutes? Convictions? Opinions? Questions?

For Further Study

General Resources
These resources will be helpful for further study of all the topics covered throughout this book.

Douglas, J. D. *The New Bible Dictionary*. 2nd ed. Wheaton, IL: Tyndale, 1982.

_____, *The New International Dictionary of the Christian Church*. Rev. ed. Grand Rapids, MI: Zondervan, 1978.

Driscoll, Mark, and Gerry Breshears. *Doctrine: What Christians Should Believe*. Wheaton, IL: Crossway, 2010.

Elwell, Walter, ed. *Evangelical Dictionary of Theology*. 2nd ed. Grand Rapids, MI: Baker Academic, 2001.

_____, ed. *Topical Analysis of the Bible: With the New International Version*. Grand Rapids, MI: Baker, 1991.

Erickson, Millard, J. *Christian Theology*. 2nd ed. Grand Rapids, MI: Eerdmans, 1998.

_____. *The Concise Dictionary of Christian Theology*. Rev. ed. Wheaton, IL: Crossway, 2001.

Grudem, Wayne. *Systematic Theology: An Introduction to Biblical Doctrine*. Grand Rapids, MI: Zondervan, 1995.

Holloman, Henry. *Kregel Dictionary of the Bible and Theology: Over 500 Key Theological Words and Concepts Defined and Cross-Referenced*. Grand Rapids, MI: Kregel Academic & Professional, 2005.

House, Wayne. *Charts of Christian Theology and Doctrine*. Grand Rapids, MI: Zondervan, 1992.

Packer, J. I. *Concise Theology: A Guide to Historic Christian Beliefs*. Wheaton, IL: Tyndale, 2001.

Theological Presuppositions and Method

Benson, Clarence H., and Robert J. Morgan. *Exploring Theology: A Guide for Systematic Theology and Apologetics*. Wheaton, IL: Crossway, 2007.

Davis, John Jefferson. *Foundations of Evangelical Theology*. Grand Rapids, MI: Baker, 1984.

Frame, John. *The Doctrine of the Knowledge of God*. Phillipsburg, NJ: Presbyterian and Reformed, 1987.

House, H. Wayne. *Charts of Christian Theology and Doctrine*. Grand Rapids, MI: Zondervan, 1992.

Lawrence, Michael. *Biblical Theology in the Life of the Church: A Guide for Ministry*. Wheaton, IL: Crossway, 2010.

Machen, J. Gresham. *Christianity and Liberalism*. Grand Rapids, MI: Eerdmans, 1923.

Woodbridge, John D., and Thomas E. McComiskey, eds. *Doing Theology in Today's World: Essays in Honor of Kenneth S. Kantzer*. Grand Rapids, MI: Zondervan, 1991.

HOW DOES GOD
REVEAL HIMSELF?

*"We are to believe and follow Christ in all things,
including his words about Scripture. And this means that
Scripture is to be for us what it was to him: the unique,
authoritative, and inerrant Word of God, and not merely
a human testimony to Christ, however carefully guided
and preserved by God. If the Bible is less than this to us,
we are not fully Christ's disciples."*
—James Montgomery Boice

Knowing God is the most important thing in life. God created people fundamentally for relationship with himself. This relationship depends on knowing who he is as he has revealed himself. God is personal, which means he has a mind, will, emotions, relational ability, and self-consciousness. Because he is personal, and not merely an impersonal object, God must personally reveal himself to us. He has done this in general revelation (the world) and special revelation (the Word of God).

THE INSPIRATION OF SCRIPTURE

The Bible is "God-breathed" (see 2 Tim. 3:16) and gets its true, authoritative, powerful, holy character from God himself, who inspired human authors to write exactly what he wanted them to write. Instead of merely dictating words to them, God worked through their unique personalities and circumstances. Scripture is therefore both fully human and fully divine. It is both the testimony of men to God's revelation, and divine revelation itself. "No prophecy of Scripture comes from someone's own interpretation. For no prophecy was ever produced by the will of man, but men spoke from God as they were carried along by the Holy Spirit" (2 Pet. 1:20–21). Because the Bible is God's Word in human words, it can be trusted as the definitive revelation from the mouth of God himself.

THE INERRANCY OF SCRIPTURE

The doctrine of inerrancy means that the Bible is entirely truthful and reliable in all that it affirms in its original manuscripts. Another way of saying this is that the Bible does not affirm anything that is contrary to fact. Because God is the ultimate author of the Bible, and because God is always perfectly truthful, it follows that his Word is completely truthful as well: he is the "God who never lies . . ." (Titus 1:2). It would be contrary to his character to affirm anything false. God is all-knowing, always truthful and good, and all-powerful, so he always knows and tells the truth and is able to communicate and preserve his Word. "O Lord GOD, you are God, and *your words are true*, and you have promised this good thing to your servant" (2 Sam. 7:28). "Every word of God proves true . . ." (Prov. 30:5; see Pss. 12:6; 119:42; John 17:17).

Inerrancy does not require twenty-first-century precision or scientifically technical language. The following quotation from the *Chicago Statement on Biblical Inerrancy* summarizes what inerrancy does *not* mean:

> We affirm the propriety of using inerrancy as a theological term with reference to the complete truthfulness of Scripture. We deny that it is proper to evaluate Scripture according to standards of truth and error that are alien to its usage or purpose. We further deny that inerrancy is negated by Biblical phenomena such as a lack of modern technical precision, irregularities of grammar or spelling, observational descriptions of nature, the reporting of falsehoods, the use of hyperbole and round numbers, the topical arrangement of material, variant selections of material in parallel accounts, or the use of free citations.[1]

The inerrancy of Scripture gives the believer great confidence in the Bible as his sure foundation for understanding all God wants him to know and all that he needs for godliness and eternal life.

THE CLARITY OF SCRIPTURE

The Bible itself acknowledges that some passages of Scripture are "hard to understand" (2 Pet. 3:16, referring to some aspects of Paul's letters). In general, however, with the illumination of the Spirit (2 Tim. 2:7), the teaching of the Bible is clear to all who seek understanding with the goal of knowing and obeying God. Old Testament believers were instructed to teach God's commands continually to their children with the expectation that they would understand it: "These words that I command you today shall be on your heart. You shall teach them diligently to your children, and shall talk of them when you sit in your house,

---

[1] Chicago Statement on Biblical Inerrancy, art. 8.

and when you walk by the way, and when you lie down, and when you rise" (Deut. 6:6–7). God's Word is said to "make wise the simple" (Ps. 19:7; see 119:30). Jesus based his teaching squarely on the Old Testament Scriptures: he assumed its teaching was clear and would often ask, "Have you not read . . . ?" (see Matt. 12:3, 5; 19:4; 21:42; 22:31).

Because of the basic clarity of the Bible, when we disagree over the meaning of a passage, they can assume that the problem is not with the Bible but rather with us as interpreters. Misunderstandings may be due to various factors such as human sin, ignorance of enough of the relevant data, faulty assumptions, or trying to reach a definite conclusion about a topic for which the Bible has not given enough information to decide the question. The Bible is mostly clear, and ordinary people are capable of comprehending Scripture for themselves. In addition, God provides teachers of his Word to further help people's understanding (1 Cor. 12:28; Eph. 4:11). Believers have the responsibility to read, interpret, and understand the Bible because it is basically clear. This was an assumption of the Protestant Reformers who sought to translate the Bible into the language of the common people. They believed that all true Christians are priests who are able to know God for themselves through his Word and to help others do the same.

THE SUFFICIENCY OF SCRIPTURE

Scripture provides all the words from God that we need in order to know God truly and personally and to live abundant, godly lives (Ps. 19:7–9; 2 Tim. 3:15). God has given his people a sufficient revelation of himself so that they are able to know, trust, and obey him. "All Scripture is breathed out by God and profitable for teaching, for reproof, for correction, and for training in righteousness, that the man of God may be competent, equipped for every good work" (2 Tim. 3:16–17). God commands that nothing be added or taken away from the Bible, which indicates that it has always been exactly what he has wanted at each stage in its development throughout the history of salvation. "You shall not add to the word that I command you, nor take from it, that you may keep the commandments of the LORD your God that I command you" (Deut. 4:2; see Deut. 12:32; Prov. 30:5–6). The powerful admonition against tampering that stands at the conclusion of the entire Bible applies primarily, of course, to the book of Revelation, but in a secondary sense what it says may be applied to the Bible as a whole: "I warn everyone who hears the words of the prophecy of this book: if anyone adds to them, God will add to him the plagues described in this book, and if anyone takes away from the words of the book of this prophecy, God will take away his share in the tree of life and in the holy city, which are described in this book" (Rev. 22:18–19).

We should find freedom and encouragement in the knowledge that God has provided all of the absolutely authoritative instruction that we need in order to know him and live as he intends. God's people should never fear that he has withheld something they might need him to say in order for them to know how to please him, or that he will have to somehow supplement his Word with new instructions for some new situation that arises in the modern age. The New Testament allows for the activity of the Holy Spirit in leading and guiding individuals, as in Rom. 8:14; Gal. 5:16, 18, 25, but this guidance is always in line with Scripture, never in opposition to scriptural commands. Therefore we should be satisfied with what Scripture teaches and what it leaves unsaid. "The secret things belong to the LORD our God, but the things that are revealed belong to us and to our children forever, that we may do all the words of this law" (Deut. 29:29).

JESUS'S VIEW OF SCRIPTURE

The most convincing reason to believe that the Bible is inspired, inerrant, clear, and sufficient is that this is what Jesus believed.

His teaching assumed that the Old Testament was the authoritative Word of his Father: "Do not think that I have come to abolish the Law or the Prophets; I have not come to abolish them but to fulfill them. For truly, I say to you, until heaven and earth pass away, not an iota, not a dot, will pass from the Law until all is accomplished" (Matt. 5:17–18). Jesus referred to dozens of Old Testament persons and events and always treated Old Testament history as historically accurate. He quoted from Genesis as his Father's Word when he said, "Have you not read that he who created them from the beginning made them male and female, and said, 'Therefore a man shall leave his father and his mother and hold fast to his wife, and the two shall become one flesh'? So they are no longer two but one flesh. What therefore God has joined together, let not man separate" (Matt. 19:4–6). Jesus not only assumed that the creation story was true, he also freely quoted words from the Old Testament narrator as words that God himself "said." It is not uncommon for Jesus's theological arguments to depend on the truthfulness of the Old Testament account (Matt. 5:12; 11:23–24; 12:41–42; 24:37–39; Luke 4:25–27; 11:50–51; John 8:56–58). Jesus's view of the Old Testament as the Word of God aligns with the way the Old Testament regularly speaks of itself.

Jesus saw his entire life as a fulfillment of Scripture (Matt. 26:54; Mark 8:31). Throughout his life, Jesus used Scripture to resist temptation (Matt. 4:1–11) and to settle disputes (Matt. 19:1–12; 22:39; 27:46; Mark 7:1–13; Luke 10:25–26). At the end of his life, Jesus died quoting Scripture (see Matt. 27:46 with Ps. 22:1). On his resurrection day he explained Scripture at length on the Emmaus road and to his disciples in Jerusalem (Luke 24:13–17, 44–47).

Conscious of his identity as God the Son, Jesus saw his teaching as no less divinely inspired than the Old Testament. Jesus taught with an authority that distinguished him from other teachers of the law. He interpreted the law on his own authority rather than depending on rabbinic sources (Matt. 5:21–48). He described his teaching and the law as sharing the same permanence: "Heaven and earth will pass away, but my words will not pass away" (Matt. 24:35; see Matt. 5:17–18; John 14:10, 24). Jesus viewed both the Old Testament and his own teaching as the Word of God. The New Testament apostolic witness was a result of Jesus's giving his disciples authority and power through the Holy Spirit to impart spiritual truths in writing no less than by word of mouth (Mark 3:13–19; John 16:12–14; Acts 26:16–18; 1 Cor. 2:12–13).

Jesus took Scripture to be the authoritative Word of God upon which he based his entire life. Those who follow Christ are called to treat Scripture (Old Testament and New Testament together) in the same way. For Christians, the Bible is a source of great delight and joy. God is to be diligently sought in his Word (1 Pet. 2:2). The Word of God is a precious treasure that deserves to be studied, meditated upon, and obeyed:

> My son, if you receive my words
>   and treasure up my commandments with you,
> making your ear attentive to wisdom
>   and inclining your heart to understanding;
> yes, if you call out for insight
>   and raise your voice for understanding,
> if you seek it like silver
>   and search for it as for hidden treasures,
> then you will understand the fear of the LORD
>   and find the knowledge of God. (Prov. 2:1–5)

SCRIPTURE MEMORY AND MEDITATION

"All Scripture is breathed out by God and profitable for teaching, for reproof, for correction, and for training

*in righteousness, that the man of God may be compe-
tent, equipped for every good work." (2 Tim. 3:16–17)*

Questions for Application and Discussion

1. What would you know about God if all you had
   was general revelation (creation)? How does special
   revelation (God's Word) help you interpret creation
   and contribute to your understanding of God? How
   does Romans 1:18–20 help you to think through these
   questions?

2. How should an understanding of the Bible as God's
   very words affect the way you devote yourself to knowing and obeying it? Why do you think there is often a
   disparity between what Christians believe about the
   Bible and their willingness to study and submit to it?

3. If there were any errors in the Bible, even small ones,
   how would that affect your trust in it? If God inspired
   Scripture and it had errors, what would that imply
   about God? What effect has denying inerrancy had on
   those churches that have done so? If you believe that
   the Bible is true in everything it affirms, how should
   that influence your attitude toward it?

4. If the Bible is basically clear in what it says, why does
   there seem to be so much disagreement about what it
   says, even among Christians? Why would God arrange
   things so that his Word would be misunderstood, and
   why would he entrust the interpretation of it to his
   frail people? What would it take for you to understand
   the Bible better?

5. If the Bible provides everything you need to know God
   and his will for your life, what affect will that have
   on the way you live your life? Have you ever wished

the Bible said more than it does about certain issues? Why do you think God has seemingly left so much up to his people to discern? How should Jesus's attitude toward the Bible influence his followers?

For Further Study

Beale, G. K. *The Erosion of Inerrancy in Evangelicalism: Responding to New Challenges to Biblical Authority*. Wheaton, IL: Crossway, 2008.

Hayden, Dan. *Did God Write the Bible?* Wheaton, IL: Crossway, 2010.

Helm, Paul. *The Divine Revelation: The Basic Issues*. Westchester, IL: Crossway, 1982.

Packer, J. I. *"Fundamentalism" and the Word of God*. London: Inter-Varsity Press, 1958.

Wenham, John W. *Christ and the Bible*. London: Tyndale, 1972.

White, James R. *Scripture Alone: Exploring the Bible's Accuracy, Authority, and Authenticity*. Minneapolis: Bethany, 2004.

HOW WELL CAN YOU
KNOW GOD?

In the quest to know God, it is vital to understand what knowing him really means. Methods, expectations, and attitudes in studying theology are determined by one's definition of "knowing God." Central to understanding this is the fact that God is both incomprehensible and knowable.

THE INCOMPREHENSIBILITY OF GOD

Scripture teaches that we can have a true and personal knowledge of God, but this does not mean we will ever understand him exhaustively. The Bible is clear that God is ultimately *incomprehensible to us*; that is, we can never fully comprehend his whole being. The following passages show this:

> Great is the LORD, and greatly to be praised,
>   and his greatness is unsearchable. (Ps. 145:3)

> Behold, these are but the outskirts of his ways,
>   and how small a whisper do we hear of him!

> But the thunder of his power who can understand?
> (Job 26:14)

> For my thoughts are not your thoughts,
>> neither are your ways my ways, declares the LORD.
> For as the heavens are higher than the earth,
>> so are my ways higher than your ways
>> and my thoughts than your thoughts. (Isa. 55:8–9)

> Oh, the depth of the riches and wisdom and knowledge
> of God! How unsearchable are his judgments and how
> inscrutable his ways! "For who has known the mind of the
> Lord, or who has been his counselor?" (Rom. 11:33–34;
> see Job 42:1–6; Pss. 139:6, 17–18; 147:5; Isa. 57:15; 1 Cor.
> 2:10–11; 1 Tim. 6:13–16)

These verses teach that not only is God's whole being incomprehensible but everything about him—his greatness, power, thoughts, ways, wisdom, and judgments—is well beyond human ability to fathom fully. Not only can we never know everything there is to know about God, we can never know everything there is to know about even one aspect of God's character or work.

Why God Is Incomprehensible

The main reasons for God's incomprehensibility are: (1) *God is infinite and his creatures are finite*. It is part of the definition of a creature to depend on its Creator for its very existence, and be therefore limited in all its aspects. Yet God is without limitations in every quality he possesses. This Creator/creature, infinite/finite gap will always exist. (2) *The perfect unity of all God's attributes* is far beyond the realm of human experience. God's love, wrath, grace, justice, holiness, patience, and jealousy are continually functioning in a perfectly integrated yet infinitely complex way. He is also everywhere present and fully aware of all that is happening at every moment, and wisely responding and reacting to every event. A finite creature cannot comprehend God's perfect, unified response to even two concurrent events. To imagine that God is simultaneously and perfectly aware of, and responding to, all of the adultery, murders, weddings, conversions, births, deaths, and acts of kindness and cruelty will overwhelm even the most brilliant human mind. (3) *The effects of sin* on the minds of fallen humans also greatly inhibit our ability to know God. The tendency of fallen creatures is to distort, pervert, and confuse truth and to use, or rather abuse, it for selfish ends rather than for God's glory (Rom. 1:18–26). (4) In his sovereign wisdom *God has chosen not to reveal some things*: "The secret things belong to the LORD our God, but the things that are revealed belong to us and to our children forever, that we may do all the words of this law" (Deut. 29:29). Many label it unloving for God to withhold information from his people. They wrongly believe that God should reveal everything they may want to know. Yet, as with all good fathers, God's wisdom leads him to refrain from answering all the questions his children ask him, and this contributes to his incomprehensibility.

In heaven, God's incomprehensibility will no doubt be lessened when the effects of sin no longer ravage minds and when he will most likely share some of his secrets. However, God will always be infinite and we will always be finite, so it will always be beyond human ability to know God exhaustively.

Implications of God's Incomprehensibility

Because God can never be fully known, those who seek to know God should be deeply humbled in the process, realizing that they will always have more to learn. The appropriate response to God is a heart of wonder and awe in light of his incomprehensible greatness. Christians should do all they can to cultivate hearts of wonder for the awesome God they worship. God's incomprehensibility also means that beliefs can be held with firm conviction even though they may be filled with inexplicable mystery. The Trinity, the divine and human natures of Christ, divine sovereignty and human responsibility, and many other core teachings of the Christian faith are profoundly mysterious; believing them requires a robust affirmation of the incomprehensibility of God.

THE KNOWABILITY OF GOD

The incomprehensibility of God could lead to despair or apathy in the quest to know God, but the Bible also teaches that God is knowable. While God can never be exhaustively understood, he can be known truly, personally, and sufficiently. God is personal, has definite characteristics, and has personally revealed himself so that he can be truly known. The multiplication of grace and peace in our lives is dependent on knowing God, and this knowledge provides sufficient resources for life and for becoming the people God wants us to be.

Knowledge of God in Christ should be our greatest delight (Jer. 9:23–24; 1 Cor. 2:2; Gal. 6:14). It is the basis of attaining eternal life (John 17:3); it is at the heart of life in the new covenant (Heb. 8:11–12); it was Paul's primary goal (Phil. 3:10); and it leads to godly love (1 John 4:7–8). God will never be known absolutely, but we can know things about him that are absolutely true, so much so that we can be willing to live and die for those beliefs. God has provided knowledge of himself that is personal, relational, and sufficient for fruitful, faithful, godly living. No one will ever be able to say he lacked the necessary revelation to know God and to start living as God intends.

Implications of the Knowability of God

God's personal and sufficient revelation of himself should foster solid conviction in believers. We need not live in ambiguity and uncertainty about who God is and what he demands of his creatures. The increasing influence of Eastern religions in the West, certain postmodern views of truth, and religious pluralism all emphasize God's incomprehensibility so much that he is ultimately made out to be unknowable. It then becomes impossible to say anything definitively true or false about him, and people think that the only heresy is claiming that there is any heresy at all! On the contrary, because of his gracious revelation and illumination, God can indeed be known. God's knowability should lead to eager, diligent, devoted study of God's Word so that we can understand him as he has revealed himself and avoid any false view of God that will dishonor him. We should never grow apathetic in seeking to know God, because we are in fact able and equipped to know him and to please him with our lives.

SCRIPTURE MEMORY AND MEDITATION

"May grace and peace be multiplied to you in the knowledge of God and of Jesus our Lord. His divine power has granted to us all things that pertain to life and godliness, through the knowledge of him who called us to his own glory and excellence." (2 Pet. 1:2–3)

Questions for Application and Discussion

1. Do you tend to err on the side of assuming that you've got God all figured out, or are you more likely to think he is so big and mysterious that he can never really be known? How has the tension between God's incomprehensibility and knowability helped you think about knowing God? What are sinful temptations that would cause someone to neglect either God's incomprehensibility or knowability?

2. What are things you can do to cultivate a heart of wonder for God's greatness?

3. Does it frustrate or worry you to know that you will never have God all figured out? If so, what in your thinking or character may be leading to this?

4. Have you ever thought that heaven might be boring with nothing left to learn about God? How does thinking about God's incomprehensibility and knowability affect your perception of heaven?

5. Do you ever doubt God's love for you because he has not given answers to some of your questions? Does the fact that he keeps some things secret (Deut. 29:29) make you feel like he doesn't respect or care for you? How should an understanding of God's wisdom change those attitudes?

For Further Study

Frame, John M. *The Doctrine of the Knowledge of God*. Phillipsburg, NJ: Presbyterian and Reformed, 1987.

Packer, J. I. *Knowing God*. London: InterVarsity Press, 1973, 13–37.

Tozer, A. W. *The Knowledge of the Holy*. New York: Harper and Row, 1961.

WHAT IS GOD LIKE?

"According to the weakness of our knowledge is the slightness of all our acts toward God. When we do not understand his justice, we shall presume upon him. When we are ignorant of his glorious majesty, we shall be rude with him. Unless we understand his holiness, we shall leap from sin to duty; if we are ignorant of his excellency, we shall lack humility before him. If we have not a sense of his omniscience, we shall be careless in his presence, full of roving thoughts, guilty of vain babbling as if he lacked information." —Stephen Charnock

"Without faith it is impossible to please [God] . . ." (Heb. 11:6); but it is also impossible to *have faith in God* without knowing the *character of God.* Faith is belief in God's promises, which are grounded in his character. The object of one's faith is supremely important. A massive amount of faith in an unreliable object is futile. Knowing God as he has revealed himself is *the* foundation of a fulfilled, meaningful life as God intended.

WAYS IN WHICH GOD REVEALS HIMSELF

God has revealed himself primarily in four overlapping ways: (1) actions; (2) names; (3) images; and (4) attributes, as seen in figure 6.1. God reveals himself through actions, names, and images because they carry vivid, experiential, creative, and situational power. But his attributes serve as foundational descriptions of his character.

Fig. 6.1

HOW GOD REVEALS HIMSELF

Means of Revelation	Examples
Actions	creating, judging, redeeming
Names	"Lord" (Hebrew, *YHWH* or *Yahweh*) "God Almighty" (Hebrew, *el Shadday*) "Master, Lord" (Hebrew, *'Adon*)
Images	Father, Rock, Husband, Shepherd
Attributes	holiness, goodness, love, grace, wrath

Actions of God

God shows who he is in what he does. In creating the world, God shows his power, wisdom, beauty, goodness, and prodigious creativity. After the creation of humanity God talks to, walks with, and seeks out humans, even when they lapse into rebellion against him, showing that he is relational, personal, engaged, and caring. God demonstrates his holiness, wrath, and justice when he curses human rebellion in the garden and judges the unrighteous through the flood in Noah's day. He shows his grace and mercy in establishing a covenant with Noah and Abraham. In sending his Son to live and die for humanity, he shows amazing love and compassion. Whenever God acts, we see his character displayed.

Names of God

God offers his name as a personal introduction and as a window into his character. This is why David says, "Those who know your name put their trust in you . . ." (Ps. 9:10). To know his name is to know he is trustworthy. God's act of naming himself is a profoundly gracious act of accommodation and engagement.

Among the many names for God in the Bible, there is none more important than *Yahweh* (translated "LORD"), a name that was revealed to Moses at the burning bush (Ex. 3:15). Linguistically related to the verb "I AM," *Yahweh* is packed with theological import. It most likely communicates God's self-existence, independence, self-sufficiency, eternality, and unchanging character. These transcendent qualities are powerfully complemented when God also tells Moses to refer to him as "the God of your fathers" (Ex. 3:15). God is both majestic and intimate, the great, eternal "I AM," the God who knows his children by name and keeps his covenant promises. Christian worship, discipleship, and preaching must maintain both healthy fear of the Lord *and* freedom and confidence in his presence.

Another striking and revealing name for God is "Jealous" (Hebrew, *'El qana'*). God tells Moses that he is so jealous for his glory expressed in the faithfulness of his people that "Jealous" is an appropriate name for himself. The reason God gives for his commandment against idolatry is grounded in his character as a jealous God: "For you shall worship no other god, for the LORD, whose name is Jealous, is a jealous God" (Ex. 34:14). God deserves and demands absolute, exclusive loyalty and hates spiritual adultery. In his jealous love he refuses to allow his people to be supremely devoted to anything but himself. Because he is absolutely worthy of worship, allowing his people to love anything more than him would compromise his justice *and* love.

Images of God

Images of God are analogies from daily life that serve to illustrate his attributes. Among many other images, God is: Father, King, Consuming Fire, Judge, Husband, Shepherd, Potter, Farmer, Refiner, Landowner, Lion, Bear, Light, Water, Tower, and Lamb! These amazingly diverse descriptions from a multitude of human experiences offer pictures of God that reach minds and hearts in ways that abstract definitions do not. Images, like attributes and names, must be considered in relation to one another. If certain images are emphasized at the expense of others, God's character will be misunderstood. The varied images in the Bible are all complementary to one other, and each is vital for understanding God. For example, God as the Rock points out his strength, stability, and justice, while God as Husband gives insight into his loving, faithful, committed heart for his covenant people.

The image of God as a rock is used in both the Old Testament and the New Testament. Deuteronomy 32 especially highlights God as Rock in light of Israel's unfaithfulness: "You were unmindful of *the Rock* that bore you, and you forgot the God who gave you birth" (Deut. 32:18; see Deut. 32:4, 13, 15, 30, 31). Paul uses this image as a title of strength and applies it to Christ in 1 Corinthians 10:4: "and all drank the same spiritual drink. For they drank from the spiritual Rock that followed them, and the Rock was Christ." Although the Rock (Hebrew, *tsur*) of Deuteronomy 32 is *Yahweh*, Paul applies the same title to Jesus. The Rock that followed and provided for the Israelites in the wilderness in the old covenant was the Christ who provides for the Corinthian believers in the new covenant. The Rock in the wilderness shares the same attributes as the Rock of the table, cup, and bread.

The strength and stability of the rock imagery is beautifully complemented by the tender, compassionate image of God as the husband of his people: "For your Maker is your husband, the

LORD of hosts is his name; and the Holy One of Israel is your Redeemer, the God of the whole earth he is called" (Isa. 54:5; see Jer. 2:2; Hos. 1–3). God's relational involvement with his people is so intimate and personal that he is jealous when his people are unfaithful. God speaks with the jealous love of a husband who has been betrayed by an adulterous wife: "Surely, as a treacherous wife leaves her husband, so have you been treacherous to me, O house of Israel, declares the LORD" (Jer. 3:20). The idea of God as a rock could lead to impersonal, static, cold conceptions, were it not for the intensely loving husband imagery. The marriage metaphor could reduce God to being weak, vulnerable, and pathetic if not for images like a rock (and a king, warrior, fire, etc.). Images of God like these bring his attributes from being mere abstractions into vivid clarity because they are based on our experiences of everyday life.

Attributes of God

The attributes of God are the normative descriptions that images, names, and actions illuminate from different perspectives. His attributes are his essential characteristics that make him who he is. God's attributes are typically classified as either incommunicable or communicable. Incommunicable attributes are shared by humans in much lesser degree than communicable attributes. Figure 6.1 shows how some of God's incommunicable attributes and his communicable attributes can be classified.

Fig. 6.2

GOD'S ATTRIBUTES

Independence (self-existence, self-sufficiency, aseity)
Unchangeableness (immutability)
Eternity
Omnipresence
Unity (simplicity)

Attributes Describing God's Being
- Spirituality
- Indivisibility

Mental Attributes
- Knowledge (omniscience)
- Truthfulness (faithfulness)

Moral Attributes
- Goodness
- Love
- Mercy (grace, patience)
- Holiness
- Peace (or order)
- Righteousness or Justice
- Jealousy
- Wrath

Attributes of Purpose
- Will
- Freedom
- Omnipotence (sovereignty)

Summary Attributes
- Perfection
- Blessedness
- Beauty
- Glory

THE UNITY OF GOD

Listing and classifying God's attributes can help develop an organized perspective on God's character. However, his character cannot be reduced to a quantifiable list of properties. Maintaining the unity of God's attributes is essential in the study of his character. His unity means that although we experience certain attributes more clearly at certain times, his attributes are not divided into parts and must always be understood interdependently. His attributes are not petals on a flower to be plucked off and viewed in isolation from the rest. The unity of God requires finite creatures to pursue a holistic understanding of him. When

God expresses judgment and wrath, he does not cease to be merciful, patient, or kind in that moment. He never expresses certain attributes at the expense of others. Fallen humans tend to emphasize attributes that affirm our personal inclinations, experience, and contemporary sensibilities. Considering God's attributes independently of one other leads to unbalanced idolatrous conceptions of God. A biblically integrated understanding of God involves, along with a list of attributes, the work of the Spirit, the whole counsel of God's Word accurately interpreted, the input of church history, and the input of believers from diverse cultures.

APPLICATION TO LIFE

Figure 6.3 provides a brief survey of some of God's attributes and the practical implications they have on our lives. The chart provides a basic definition of an attribute, a key passage of supporting Scripture, and one basic implication for daily life.[1]

GOD'S ATTRIBUTES ARE SEEN MOST CLEARLY IN CHRIST

Jesus Christ is the most definitive revelation of the divine attributes. To see God's character we look ultimately to God incarnate: "For God, who said, 'Let light shine out of darkness,' has shone in our hearts to give the light of the knowledge of the glory of God in the face of Jesus Christ" (2 Cor. 4:6). In the cross of Christ all God's major attributes are displayed in condensed lucidity. His wrath, grace, justice, mercy, sovereignty, goodness, love, holiness, compassion, wisdom, and power meet in Christ for the world to see. When discussions of God's attributes become esoteric and sterile, it is the face and cross of Christ that restores radical clarity, reality, and compelling beauty.

---

[1] Figure 6.3 is based on Wayne Grudem's *Systematic Theology* (Grand Rapids, MI: Zondervan), 1994.

Fig. 6.3

PRACTICAL IMPLICATIONS OF GOD'S ATTRIBUTES

Attribute	Scripture	Implication
Independence: God does not need us or the rest of creation for anything, yet we and the rest of creation can glorify him and bring him joy.	"The God who made the world and everything in it, being Lord of heaven and earth, does not live in temples made by man, nor is he served by human hands, as though he needed anything, since he himself gives to all mankind life and breath and everything." (Acts 17:24–25; see Ex. 3:14; Job 41:11; Pss. 50:9–12; 90:2)	God never experiences need, so serving God should never be motivated by the thought that he needs us. He is the provider in everything.
Immutability: God is unchanging in his being, perfections, purposes, and promises, although as he acts in response to different situations, he feels emotions.	"For I the LORD do not change; therefore you, O children of Jacob, are not consumed" (Mal. 3:6; for "being" see Ps. 102:25–27; Mal. 3:6; James 1:17; for "purposes" see Ps. 33:11; Isa. 46:9–11; for "promises" see Num. 23:19; Rom. 11:29)	God can always be trusted, because he always keeps his word, and he is never capricious or moody.
Eternity: God has no beginning or end and is in no way bound by time, although he sees events and acts in his world in time, which is in fact one dimension of the created order.	"Before the mountains were brought forth, or ever you had formed the earth and the world, from everlasting to everlasting you are God." (Ps. 90:2; see Ex. 3:14; Job 36:26; Ps. 90:4; Isa. 46:9–10; John 8:58; 1 Tim. 6:16; 2 Pet. 3:8; Jude 24–25; Rev. 1:8; 4:8)	Those who trust the God of eternity can know peace, rest, and comfort in the busyness of life and in spite of impending death, for God keeps them in safety and joy forever.

Attribute	Scripture	Implication
Omnipresence: God does not have spatial dimensions and is present everywhere with his whole being, though he acts differently in different situations.	"Am I a God at hand, declares the LORD, and not a God far away? Can a man hide himself in secret places so that I cannot see him? declares the LORD. Do I not fill heaven and earth? . . ." (Jer. 23:23–24; see 1 Kings 8:27; Ps. 139:7–10; Isa. 66:1–2; Acts 7:48–50)	God can be sought anywhere regardless of place. Believers should never feel lonely, and the wicked should never feel safe.
Holiness: God is absolutely and uniquely excellent above all creation (majesty) and without sin (purity).	"And the four living creatures, each of them with six wings, are full of eyes all around and within, and day and night they never cease to say, 'Holy, holy, holy, is the Lord God Almighty, who was and is and is to come!'" (Rev. 4:8; for "majestic holiness" see Ex. 15:11; 1 Chron. 16:27–29; Isa. 57:15; for "moral holiness" see Isa. 5:16; 6:1–8; Acts 3:14; Heb. 7:26)	God should be feared and obeyed, and his people should earnestly pursue moral purity.
Omnipotence: God is able to do all his holy will.	"Remember the former things of old; for I am God, and there is no other; I am God, and there is none like me, declaring the end from the beginning and from ancient times things not yet done, saying, 'My counsel shall stand, and I will accomplish all my purpose.'" (Isa. 46:9–10; see Ex. 6:3; Job 37:23; 40:2; 42:1–6; Pss. 33:10–11; 91:1; Dan. 4:34–35; Matt. 28:18)	God's ultimate will is never frustrated by evil, so there is peace and confidence in the face of suffering for those who trust God.

Attribute	Scripture	Implication
Sovereignty: God has absolute rule over creation as King and total control and determination over all that happens.	"His dominion is an ever-lasting dominion, and his kingdom endures from generation to generation; all the inhabitants of the earth are accounted as nothing, and he does according to his will among the host of heaven and among the inhabitants of the earth; and none can stay his hand or say to him, 'What have you done?'" (Dan. 4:34–35; see 1 Chron. 29:11–13; Pss. 22:28; 24:1; 47:7–9; 103:19; Prov. 16:33; Dan. 4:25; 7:1–28; 12:1–13; Matt. 6:13; 10:29; Acts 17:26; Eph. 1:11; 1 Tim. 6:15; James 1:13–15)	Mankind should obey and submit to God as humble subjects of his kingdom.
Omniscience: God fully knows himself and all things actual and possible—past, present, and future.	"Whenever our heart condemns us, God is greater than our heart, and he knows everything." (1 John 3:20; see Job 28:24; 37:16; Pss. 139:1–3; 147:5; Isa. 55:8–9; Matt. 10:29–30; Rom. 11:33–34; 1 Cor. 2:10–11; Heb. 4:13)	All God's thoughts and actions are perfectly informed by perfect knowledge, so he is perfectly trustworthy.
Wisdom: God always knows and chooses the best goals and the best means to those goals. Wisdom is a moral as well as an intellectual quality.	"Blessed be the name of God forever and ever, to whom belong wisdom and might." (Dan. 2:20; see Job 9:4; 12:13; Ps. 104:24; Rom. 11:33; 16:27; 1 Cor. 1:21–29; Eph. 3:10–11)	God's wisdom is not always clear to us, but it is great, deep, and valuable, and it should be highly desired and sought. We should not doubt its reality even in circumstances that upset us.

Attribute	Scripture	Implication
Love: God freely and eternally gives of himself. The ultimate historical demonstration of God's love is seen in the cross of Christ.	"Anyone who does not love does not know God, because God is love. In this the love of God was made manifest among us, that God sent his only Son into the world, so that we might live through him. In this is love, not that we have loved God but that he loved us and sent his Son to be the propitiation for our sins." (1 John 4:8–10; see John 3:16; 15:13; 17:24; Rom. 5:8; 8:31–39; Gal. 2:20; 1 John 3:16; 4:16)	God is eager to extravagantly give of himself to meet the needs of lost sinners, so they should flee to him with confidence (see Rom. 8:32).
Wrath: God intensely hates and responds with anger to all sin and rebellion. God hates every threat to what he loves.	"Then the kings of the earth and the great ones and the generals and the rich and the powerful, and everyone, slave and free, hid themselves in the caves and among the rocks of the mountains, calling to the mountains and rocks, 'Fall on us and hide us from the face of him who is seated on the throne, and from the wrath of the Lamb.'" (Rev. 6:15–16; see Ex. 34:7; Rom. 1:18; 2:4; 2 Cor. 5:10; 2 Thess. 1:5; 2 Pet. 3:9)	God should be greatly feared. Unbelievers should fear his judgment and turn to Christ for salvation. Believers should fear God's fatherly discipline. The God who loves us is also the holy God who hates sin (1 Pet. 1:17).

SCRIPTURE MEMORY AND MEDITATION

"The Lord passed before him and proclaimed, "'The Lord, the Lord, a God merciful and gracious, slow to anger, and abounding in steadfast love and faithful-

ness, keeping steadfast love for thousands, forgiving iniquity and transgression and sin, but who will by no means clear the guilty, visiting the iniquity of the fathers on the children and the children's children, to the third and the fourth generation.'" (Ex. 34:6–7)

Questions for Application and Discussion

1. Can you see how all of life's greatest problems originate in a faulty understanding of who God is?

2. What attribute of God is especially meaningful to you? Are there experiences in your life that have made this attribute take on its significance?

3. Is there an attribute of God that most troubles or confuses you? What is the source of this difficulty?

4. Has your experience in life and knowledge of the Scriptures helped you to develop a biblically balanced understanding of God's attributes in a unified way? If not, what attributes have been neglected?

5. What steps could you take to develop a better understanding of God's character? Are there sections of the Bible you have neglected that might help?

For Further Study

Carson, D. A. *The Difficult Doctrine of the Love of God*. Wheaton, IL: Crossway, 1999.

Coppedge, Allen. *Portraits of God: A Biblical Theology of Holiness*. Downers Grove, IL: InterVarsity, 2001.

Feinberg, John. *No One Like Him: The Doctrine of God*. Wheaton, IL: Crossway, 2006.

Frame, John. *The Doctrine of God: A Theology of Lordship*. Phillipsburg, NJ: P&R, 2002.

Packer, J. I. *Knowing God*. London: Inter-Varsity Press, 1973.

Piper, John. *Desiring God*. Rev. ed. Portland, OR: Multnomah, 2003.

———. *The Pleasures of God*. Rev. ed. Portland, OR: Multnomah, 2000.

Sproul, R. C. *The Holiness of God*. Carol Stream, IL: Tyndale, 2000.

Thoennes, K. Erik. *Godly Jealousy: A Theology of Intolerant Love*. Scotland: Christian Focus/Mentor, 2008.

Tozer, A. W. *The Knowledge of the Holy*. New York: HarperOne, 1978.

Ware, Bruce A. *God's Greater Glory: The Exalted God of Scripture and the Christian Faith*. Wheaton, IL: Crossway, 2004.

HOW DO YOU EXPLAIN THE TRINITY?

"God has appeared glorious to me, on account of the Trinity." —Jonathan Edwards

The biblical teaching on the Trinity is summarized with four essential affirmations:

1. There is one—and only one—true and living God.
2. This one God eternally exists in three persons—God the Father, God the Son, and God the Holy Spirit.
3. These three persons are completely equal in attributes, each having the same divine nature.
4. While each person is *fully* and *completely* God, the persons are not identical.

The differences among Father, Son, and Holy Spirit are found in the way they relate to one another and the role each plays in accomplishing their unified purpose.

The unity of nature and distinction of persons of the Trinity is helpfully illustrated in figure 7.1.

Fig. 7.1

THE TRINITY

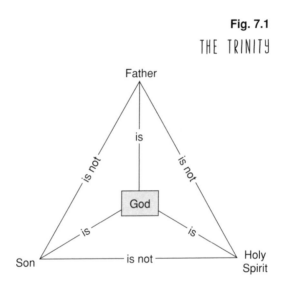

GOD IS ONE GOD: MONOTHEISM

There is nothing more fundamental to biblical theology than monotheism (the biblical belief that there is one, and only one, God): "Hear, O Israel: the LORD our God, the LORD is one" (Deut. 6:4). This verse, known as the *Shema* in Hebrew (from the opening verb of the verse meaning "hear" or "listen"), is one of the most familiar and foundational verses in the Old Testament. God rejects polytheism (belief in many gods) and demands exclusive devotion: "I am the LORD, and there is no other, besides me there is no God . . ." (Isa. 45:5; see Deut. 4:35, 39; 1 Kings 8:60; Isa. 40:18; 46:9). The New Testament affirms the deity of the Father,

Son, and Holy Spirit, as we shall see, but does not waver from Old Testament monotheism (John 17:3; 1 Cor. 8:4–6; 1 Tim. 2:5; James 2:19). Jesus quotes the *Shema* in a debate with the Jewish leaders (Mark 12:29), and Paul continues to teach that there is one God while recognizing Jesus as the divine-human Mediator between God and man (1 Tim. 2:5).

Implications of Monotheism

Because there is only one God, idolatry of any kind is evil, foolish, wrong, and harmful. Worship of other "gods" robs the true God of the devotion and glory he alone deserves. Idolatry can take many forms. Idols are not only man-made objects; an idol is *anything* allowed to compete with God for our ultimate loyalty. According to Jesus, money can become an idol: "You cannot serve God and money" (Matt. 6:24). Greed, lust, and impurity can be indicators of idolatry (Eph. 5:5; Col. 3:5). Idolatry is foolish, deceptive, and dangerous—and may even involve demonic activity (1 Cor. 10:19–20).

Because there is only one God, he alone should be the ultimate object of our affections. He alone deserves absolute allegiance and obedience. The Great Commandment that follows the *Shema* is the obvious implication of monotheism: "You shall love the Lord your God with all your heart and with all your soul and with all your might" (Deut. 6:5). The one true God deserves all we are and have. He deserves wholehearted love because nothing compares with him.

GOD IS THREE PERSONS: THE TRI-UNITY OF GOD

As the nature of God is progressively revealed in Scripture, the one God is seen to exist eternally in three persons. These three persons share the same divine nature yet are different in role and relationship. The basic principle at the heart of God's triune being is *unity* and *distinction*, both coexisting without either being compromised. Anything that is necessarily true of God is true of Father, Son, and Spirit. They are equal in essence yet distinct in function and how they relate to one another.

The doctrine of the Trinity is most fully realized in the New Testament, where the divine Father, Son, and Spirit are seen accomplishing redemption (Heb. 9:14). But while the New Testament gives the clearest picture of the Trinity, there are hints within the Old Testament of what is yet to come. In the beginning of the Bible, the Spirit of God is "hovering over the face of the waters" at creation (Gen. 1:2). And the Spirit is elsewhere described as a personal being, possessing the attributes of God and yet distinct from Yahweh (Isa. 48:16; 61:1; 63:10). Some interpreters think that the plurality within God is seen in the Hebrew word for God, 'Elohim, which is plural in form (though some think that this is insignificant; the word is used with singular verbs, and all agree that it has a singular meaning in the Old Testament). In addition, the use of plural pronouns when God refers to himself hints at a plurality of persons: "Then God said, 'Let us make man in our image . . .'" (Gen. 1:26; see Gen. 3:22; 11:7; Isa. 6:8). The plurality of God may also be seen in humans made in his image; people share the same human nature, yet are made distinct in role and relationship as male and female: "So God created man in his own image, in the image of God he created him; male and female he created them" (Gen. 1:27).

The plurality of God also seems to be indicated when the Angel of the Lord appears in the Old Testament as one who represents Yahweh, while at times this Angel seems to be no different in attributes or actions from God himself (see Gen. 16:7, 10–11, 13; 18:1–33; Ex. 3:1–4:31; Num. 22:35, 38; Judg. 2:1–2; 6:11–18). There are also passages in the Old Testament that call two persons God or Lord: "Your throne, O God, is forever and ever. The scepter of your kingdom is a scepter of uprightness; you have loved righteousness and hated wickedness. Therefore

God, your God, has anointed you with the oil of gladness above your companions" (Ps. 45:6–7). David says, "The LORD says to my Lord: 'Sit at my right hand, until I make your enemies your footstool'" (Ps. 110:1). The God who is set above his companions (Ps. 45:7) and the Lord of Psalm 110:1 are recognized as Christ in the New Testament (Heb. 1:8, 13). Christ himself applies Psalm 110:1 to himself (Matt. 22:41–46). Other passages give divine status to a messianic figure distinct from Yahweh (Prov. 8:22–31; 30:4; Dan. 7:13–14).

The Old Testament glimpses of God's plurality blossom into the full picture of the Trinity in the New Testament, where the deity and distinct persons of Father, Son, and Spirit function together in perfect unity and equality (on the deity of Christ and the Holy Spirit, see the next two chapters, "Who Is Jesus Christ?"and "Who Is the Holy Spirit?"). Perhaps the clearest picture of this distinction and unity is Jesus's baptism, where the Son is anointed for his public ministry by the Spirit, descending as a dove, with the Father declaring from heaven, "This is my beloved Son, with whom I am well pleased" (Matt. 3:17). All three persons of the Trinity are present, and each one is doing something different.

The New Testament authors employ a Trinitarian cadence as they write about the work of God. Prayers of blessing and descriptions of gifts within the body of Christ are Trinitarian in nature: "The grace of the Lord Jesus Christ and the love of God and the fellowship of the Holy Spirit be with you all" (2 Cor. 13:14); "Now there are varieties of gifts, but the same Spirit; and there are varieties of service, but the same Lord; and there are varieties of activities, but it is the same God who empowers them all in everyone" (1 Cor. 12:4–6). The persons of the Trinity are also linked in the baptismal formula of Matthew 28:19, "baptizing them in [or into] the name of the Father and of the Son and of the Holy Spirit." There are many other passages that reveal the Trinitarian, or at least the plural, nature of God (e.g., John 14:16, 26; 16:13–15; 20:21–22; Rom. 8:9; 15:16, 30; 2 Cor. 1:21–22; Gal. 4:4–6; Eph. 2:18; 4:4–6; 1 Pet. 1:1–2; 1 John 4:2, 13–14; Jude 20–21).

Differences in roles also appear consistently in biblical testimonies concerning the relationships between Father, Son, and Holy Spirit. The uniform pattern of Scripture is that the Father plans, directs, and sends; the Son is sent by the Father and is subject to the Father's authority and obedient to the Father's will; and both Father and Son direct and send the Spirit, who carries out the will of both. Yet this is somehow consistent with equality in being and in attributes. The Father created through the Son (John 1:3; 1 Cor. 8:6; Col. 1:16; Heb. 1:2), and the Father planned redemption and sent the Son into the world (John 3:16; Rom. 8:29; Gal. 4:4; Eph. 1:3–5). The Son obeyed the Father and accomplished redemption for us (John 4:34; 5:19; 6:38; Heb. 10:5–7; see Matt. 26:64; Acts 2:33; 1 Cor. 15:28; Heb. 1:3). The Father did not come to die for our sins, nor did the Holy Spirit, but that was the role of the Son. The Father and Son both send the Holy Spirit in a new way after Pentecost (John 14:26; 15:26; 16:7). These relationships existed eternally (Rom. 8:29; Eph. 1:4; Rev. 13:8), and they provide the basis for simultaneous equality and differences in various human relationships. The believer's identification with the redeeming work of the Trinity is seen in the baptismal formula of Matt. 28:19: ". . . baptizing them in the name [one name] of the Father and of the Son and of the Holy Spirit [three persons]. . . ."

Within God there is both unity and diversity: unity without uniformity, and diversity without division. The early church saw this Trinitarian balance clearly. For example, the Athanasian Creed (c. AD 500) says:

> We worship one God in the Trinity and the Trinity in unity;
> we distinguish among the persons, but we do not divide the

> substance. . . . The entire three persons are co-eternal and
> co-equal with one another, so that . . . we worship complete
> unity in Trinity and Trinity in unity.

This unity and diversity is at the heart of the great mystery of the Trinity. Unity without uniformity is baffling to finite minds, but the world shows different types of reflections of this principle of oneness and distinction at every turn. What is the source of the transcendent beauty in a symphony, the human body, marriage, ecosystems, the church, the human race, a delicious meal, or a perfectly executed fast break in basketball? Is it not, in large part, due to the distinct parts coming together to form a unified whole, leading to a unified result? Unity and distinction—the principle at the heart of the Trinity—can be seen in much of what makes life so rich and beautiful. Woven into the fabric of the world are multiple reflections of the One who made it with unity and distinction as the parallel qualities of its existence.

HISTORICAL MISUNDERSTANDINGS OF THE TRINITY

One of the most fundamental ways to misunderstand the Trinity is *tritheism*, which understands the distinction between the persons of the Trinity so you have three different gods. This view neglects the oneness of the natures of Father, Son, and Holy Spirit. At the other end of the spectrum is the heresy of *modalism* (also known as Sabellianism, named after its earliest proponent, Sabellius, of the third century), which loses the distinctions between the persons and claims that God is only one person. In this view, the appearance of the three persons is merely three *modes* of existence of the one God. For instance, God reveals himself as Father when he is creating and giving the law, as Son in redemption, and as Spirit in the church age. A contemporary version of modalism is found in the teaching of

Oneness Pentecostalism. Both tritheism and modalism fail to maintain the biblical balance between the oneness of God and his eternal existence in three persons. A third error is to deny the full deity of the Son and of the Holy Spirit, and to say that they were at some time created. This is the heresy of *Arianism* (named after a teacher, Arius, c. AD 256–336), which is held today by Jehovah's Witnesses.

PRACTICAL IMPLICATIONS OF THE TRINITY

What are some of the practical implications of the doctrine of the Trinity?

1. The doctrine of the Trinity makes definitive revelation of God possible as he is known in Christ: "No one has ever seen God; the only God, who is at the Father's side, he has made him known" (John 1:18). No man can see God and live (Ex. 33:20; 1 Tim. 6:16), but God the Son provided an actual manifestation of God in the flesh.

2. The Trinity makes the atonement possible. Redemption of sinful man is accomplished through the distinct and unified activity of each person of the Godhead: "How much more will the blood of *Christ*, who through the eternal *Spirit* offered himself without blemish to *God*, purify our conscience from dead works to serve the living God" (Heb. 9:14).

3. Because God is triune, he has eternally been personal and relational in his own being, in full independence from his creation. God has never had any unmet needs, "nor is he served by human hands, as though he needed anything, since he himself gives to all mankind life and breath and everything" (Acts 17:25). Personhood becomes real only within realized relationships, and the reality of relationship can only exist where one has something or someone that is not oneself to relate to; if, then, God had not been plural in himself, he could not have been a personal, relational God until he had begun creating, and thus he

would have been dependent on creation for his own personhood, which is a notion as nonsensical as it is unscriptural. Between the persons of the Trinity, there has always existed total relational harmony and expression. Apart from the plurality in the Trinity, either God's eternal independence from the created order or his eternally relational personal existence would have to be denied.

4. The Trinity provides the ultimate model for relationships within the body of Christ and marriage (1 Cor. 11:3; 12:4–6; Eph. 4:4–7).

The doctrine of the Trinity is well beyond human ability to ever fully comprehend. However, it is central to understanding the nature of God and the central events in the history of salvation. Biblical Christianity stands or falls with the doctrine of the Trinity.

SCRIPTURE MEMORY AND MEDITATION

"How much more will the blood of Christ, who through the eternal Spirit offered himself without blemish to God, purify our conscience from dead works to serve the living God." (Heb. 9:14)

Questions for Application and Discussion

1. What are some examples of how we see "unity and distinction" in everyday life? What things in life especially delight you when you see diverse parts functioning in harmonious ways?

2. How could a good understanding of the unity without uniformity in the Trinity help marriages? Fellowship in the church? Appreciation for different cultures? Missions? Music? Sports?

3. How would you explain the difference between tritheism, modalism, and the Trinity?

4. How does the Trinity affect our lives in practical ways?

5. Does your inability to fully understand the doctrine of Trinitarianism cause you to doubt or be frustrated? Why would it make sense for something so central to the nature of God to be well beyond our ability to fully figure out?

For Further Study

Kostenberger, Andreas J., and Scott R. Swain. *Father, Son, and Spirit: The Trinity and John's Gospel*. New Studies in Biblical Theology. Downers Grove, IL: InterVarsity Academic, 2008.

Letham, Robert. *The Holy Trinity: In Scripture, History, Theology, and Worship*. Phillipsburg, NJ: P&R, 2005.

McGrath, Alister E. *Understanding the Trinity*. Grand Rapids, MI: Zondervan, 1988.

Owen, John. *Communion with the Triune God*. Edited by Kelly M. Kapic and Justin Taylor. Wheaton, IL: Crossway, 2007.

Packer, J. I. *Knowing God*. Downers Grove, IL: InterVarsity. Twentieth anniversary ed. 1993.

Sanders, Fred. *The Deep Things of God: How the Trinity Changes Everything*. Wheaton, IL: Crossway, 2010.

Sanders, Fred, and Klaus Issler, eds. *Jesus in Trinitarian Perspective: An Introductory Christology*. Nashville: B&H Academic, 2007.

Ware, Bruce. *Father, Son, and Holy Spirit: Relationships, Roles, and Relevance*. Wheaton, IL: Crossway, 2005.

White, James R. *The Forgotten Trinity: Recovering the Heart of Christian Belief*. Minneapolis: Bethany, 1998.

WHO IS JESUS CHRIST?

"There is no mystery in heaven or earth so great as this—a suffering deity, an almighty Savior nailed to the Cross." —Samuel M. Zwemer

Four statements must be understood and affirmed in order to attain a complete biblical picture of the person of Jesus Christ:

1. Jesus Christ is fully and completely divine.
2. Jesus Christ is fully and completely human.
3. The divine and human natures of Christ are distinct.
4. The divine and human natures of Christ are completely united in one person.

THE DEITY OF CHRIST

Many passages of Scripture demonstrate that Jesus is fully and completely God:

In the beginning was the Word, and the Word was with God, and *the Word was God*. . . . And the Word became flesh and dwelt among us, and we have seen his glory, glory as of the only Son from the Father, full of grace and truth. (John 1:1, 14)

No one has ever seen God; the only God, who is at the Father's side, he has made him known. (John 1:18)

Thomas answered him, "My Lord and my God!" (John 20:28)

To them belong the patriarchs, and from their race, according to the flesh, is the *Christ who is God over all*, blessed forever. Amen. (Rom. 9:5)

Have this mind among yourselves, which is yours in Christ Jesus, who, though he was *in the form of God*, did not count *equality with God* a thing to be grasped, but made himself nothing, taking the form of a servant, being born in the likeness of men. (Phil. 2:5–7)

Waiting for our blessed hope, the appearing of the glory of *our great God* and Savior Jesus Christ. (Titus 2:13)

He is the radiance of the glory of God and the exact imprint of his nature, and he upholds the universe by the word of his power. . . . (Heb. 1:3)

But of the Son he says,
    "Your throne, O God, is forever and ever." . . .

And,

    "You, Lord, laid the foundation of the earth in the
        beginning,
and the heavens are the work of your hands." (Heb. 1:8, 10)

Simeon Peter, a servant and apostle of Jesus Christ,
To those who have obtained a faith of equal standing with ours by the righteousness of our God and Savior Jesus Christ. (2 Pet. 1:1)

Jesus's Understanding of His Own Deity

Even though the passages cited above clearly teach the deity of Christ, this truth is often challenged. Some say that Jesus never claimed to be God and that these verses were written by his disciples who deified him because of the impact he had on their lives. Some claim that Jesus saw himself only as a great moral teacher on a par with other religious leaders. However, in the Gospels Jesus's understanding of his own deity does not support this perspective. He clearly saw himself as God. We see this primarily in six ways.

1. Jesus taught with *divine authority*. At the end of the Sermon on the Mount, "the crowds were astonished at his teaching, for he was *teaching them as one who had authority*, and not as their scribes" (Matt. 7:28–29). The teachers of the law in Jesus's day had no authority of their own. Their authority came from their use of earlier authorities. Even Moses and the other Old Testament prophets and authors did not speak in their own authority, but would say, "This is what the Lord says." Jesus, on the other hand, interprets the law by saying, "You have heard that it was said. . . . But *I say to you*" (see Matt. 5:22, 28, 32, 34, 39, 44). This divine authority is shown with staggering clarity when he speaks of himself as the Lord who will judge the whole earth and will say to the wicked, "I never knew you; depart from me, you workers of lawlessness" (Matt. 7:23). No wonder the crowd was amazed at the authority with which Jesus spoke. Jesus recognized that his words carried divine weight. He acknowledged the permanent authority of the law (Matt. 5:18) and put his words on an equal plane with it: "For truly, I say to

you, until heaven and earth pass away, not an iota, not a dot, will pass from *the Law* until all is accomplished" (Matt. 5:18); "Heaven and earth will pass away, but *my words* will not pass away" (Matt. 24:35).

2. Jesus had a *unique relationship with God the Father*. When he was a young boy, Jesus sat with the religious leaders in the temple, amazing people with the answers he gave. When his distraught parents finally found their "lost" adolescent, he replied by saying, "Why were you looking for me? Did you not know that I must be in *my Father's* house?" (Luke 2:49). Jesus's reference to God as "my Father" is a radical statement of a unique, intimate relationship with God, of which he was already fully conscious. Such a reference by an individual was unprecedented in Jewish literature. Jesus took this unique personal address to another level by referring to God the Father using the affectionate Aramaic expression *'Abba'*.

3. Jesus's favorite self-designation was the title *Son of Man*. The phrase "a son of man" could mean merely "a human being." But Jesus refers to himself as *the* Son of Man, which indicates that he sees himself as the messianic Son of Man in Daniel 7 who is to rule over the whole world for all eternity:

> I saw in the night visions,
> and behold, with the clouds of heaven
>   there came *one like a son of man*,
> and he came to the Ancient of Days
>   and was presented before him.
> And to him was given *dominion*
>   *and glory* and a kingdom,
> that *all peoples, nations, and languages*
>   *should serve him*;
> his dominion is an *everlasting dominion*,
>   which shall not pass away,
> and his kingdom one

that shall not be destroyed. (Dan. 7:13–14)

Jesus establishes his divine authority as the glorious messianic Son of Man by declaring that he has the power to forgive sin and is Lord of the Sabbath: "'But that you may know that the *Son of Man* has authority on earth *to forgive sins*'—he said to the paralytic—'I say to you, rise, pick up your bed, and go home'" (Mark 2:10–11); "And he said to them, 'The Sabbath was made for man, not man for the Sabbath. So *the Son of Man* is *lord even of the Sabbath*'" (Mark 2:27–28).

4. Jesus's teaching emphasized *his own identity*. Jesus came teaching the kingdom of God, and in it he was the King. His teaching dealt with many topics but was centrally about himself. His question to his disciples, "But who do you say that I am?" (Matt. 16:15), is the ultimate question of his ministry.

5. Jesus *received worship*. Perhaps the most radical demonstration of Jesus's belief that he was God is the fact that when he was worshiped, as he sometimes was, he accepted that worship (Matt. 14:33; 28:9, 17; John 9:38; 20:28). If Jesus did not believe he was God, he should have vehemently rejected being worshiped, as Paul and Barnabas did in Lystra (Acts 14:14–15). That a monotheistic Jew like Jesus accepted worship from other monotheistic Jews shows that Jesus realized that he was God.

6. Jesus *equated himself with the Father*, and as a result the Jewish leaders accused him of blasphemy:

> But Jesus answered them, "My Father is working until now, and I am working."
>
> This was why the Jews were seeking all the more to kill him, because not only was he breaking the Sabbath, but he was even calling God his own Father, making himself equal with God. (John 5:17–18)

Jesus said to them, "Truly, truly, I say to you, before Abraham was, *I am*" [a clear allusion to the sacred divine name of Yahweh; see Ex. 3:14]. So they picked up stones to throw at him. . . . (John 8:58–59)

"I and the Father are one."

The Jews picked up stones again to stone him. . . . The Jews answered him, "It is not for a good work that we are going to stone you but for blasphemy, because you, being a man, *make yourself God*." (John 10:30–33)

Again the high priest asked him, "Are you the Christ, the Son of the Blessed?" And Jesus said, "I am, and you will see the *Son of Man* seated at the right hand of Power, and coming with the clouds of heaven" [a reference to Daniel 7; see point 3 above]. And the high priest tore his garments and said, "What further witnesses do we need? You have heard his *blasphemy*. What is your decision?" And they all condemned him as deserving death. (Mark 14:61–64)

Implications of Christ's Deity

Because Jesus is God, the following things are true:

1. God can be known definitively and personally in Christ: "No one has ever seen God; the only God, who is at the Father's side, he has made him known" (John 1:18); "Whoever has seen me has seen the Father . . ." (John 14:9).

2. Redemption is possible and has been accomplished in Christ: "For there is one God, and there is one mediator between God and men, the man Christ Jesus" (1 Tim. 2:5).

3. In Christ risen, ascended, and enthroned we have a sympathetic high priest who has omnipotent power to meet our needs: "For we do not have a high priest who is unable to sympathize with our weaknesses, but one who in every respect has been tempted as we are, yet without sin. Let us then with confidence draw near to the throne of grace, that we may

receive mercy and find grace to help in time of need" (Heb. 4:15–16).

4. Worship of and obedience to Christ are appropriate and necessary (Phil. 2:5–11).

Historical Misunderstandings of Christ's Deity

The earliest and most radical denial of the deity of Christ is called *Ebionism* or *Adoptionism*, which was taught by a small Jewish-Christian sect in the first century. They believed that the power of God came on a man named Jesus to enable him to fulfill the messianic role, but that Christ was not God. A later and more influential christological heresy was *Arianism* (early fourth century), which denied the eternal, fully divine nature of Christ. Arius (c. 256–336) believed Jesus was the "first and greatest of created beings." Arius's denial of Jesus's full deity was rejected at the Council of Nicea in 325. At this council, Athanasius showed that according to Scripture Jesus is fully God, being of the *same essence* as the Father.

THE HUMANITY OF CHRIST

From the moment of Mary's miraculous conception of Jesus, his divine nature became permanently united to his human nature in one and the same person, the now incarnate Son of God. The biblical evidence for Jesus's humanity is strong, showing that he had a human body and a human mind, and that he experienced human temptation.

Jesus had a *human birth* and a *human genealogy*: "But when the fullness of time had come, God sent forth his Son, born of woman, born under the law, to redeem those who were under the law, so that we might receive adoption as sons" (Gal. 4:4–5).

Jesus had a *human body* that experienced growth (Luke 2:40, 52) as well as physical susceptibilities like hunger (Matt.

4:2), thirst (John 19:28), tiredness (John 4:6), and death (Luke 23:46).

As an old man, the apostle John was still in awe of the fact that he had been able to experience God the Son in the flesh. Like an enthusiastic child, he keeps repeating himself as he describes the incarnation:

> That which was from the beginning, which we have *heard*, which we have *seen with our eyes*, which we *looked upon* and have *touched with our hands*, concerning the word of life—the life was *made manifest*, and we have *seen it*, and testify to it and proclaim to you the eternal life, which was with the Father and was made manifest to us—that which *we have seen* and *heard* we proclaim also to you, so that you too may have fellowship with us; and indeed our fellowship is with the Father and with his Son Jesus Christ. (1 John 1:1–3)

John has known about the incarnation for over fifty years when he writes this letter, yet he still writes with wide-eyed wonder as he reflects on walking the shores of Galilee, fishing, eating, laughing with, and having his feet washed by a carpenter who was God in flesh!

Jesus continues to have a physical body in his resurrected state, and he went to great lengths to make sure his disciples realized this: "See my hands and my feet, that it is I myself. Touch me, and see. For a spirit does not have flesh and bones as you see that I have" (Luke 24:39; see Luke 24:42–43; John 20:17, 25–27). After his resurrection, Jesus returned to the Father by ascending in his divinely reanimated body before his disciples' wondering eyes, thus affirming his ongoing full physical humanity (Luke 24:50–51; Acts 1:9–11). The ascension has been included in every important creed of the church because it teaches the enduring complete humanity of Jesus as the only mediator between God and man.

Jesus had a *human mind* that, in submission to the will of the Father, had limitations in knowledge: "But concerning that day or that hour, no one knows, not even the angels in heaven, nor the Son, but only the Father" (Mark 13:32). His human mind grew and increased in wisdom (Luke 2:52), and he even "learned obedience" (Heb. 5:8). To say Jesus "learned obedience" does not mean he moved from disobedience to obedience, but that he grew in his capacity to obey as he endured suffering.

Jesus experienced *human temptation*: "For we do not have a high priest who is unable to sympathize with our weaknesses, but one who in every respect has been tempted as we are, yet without sin" (Heb. 4:15; see Luke 4:1–2). While Jesus experienced every kind of human temptation, he never succumbed to sin (John 8:29, 46; 15:10; 2 Cor. 5:21; Heb. 7:26; 1 Pet. 2:22; 1 John 3:5).

Jesus practiced spiritual disciplines and grew spiritually. He regularly prayed with passion (Mark 14:36; Luke 10:21; Heb. 5:7), worshiped at services in the synagogue and temple (Luke 4:16; John 7:14), read and memorized Scripture (Matt. 4:4–10), practiced the discipline of solitude (Mark 1:35; 6:46), observed the Sabbath (Luke 4:16), obeyed the Old Testament laws (John 8:29; 15:10; 2 Cor. 5:21; Heb. 4:15), and received the fullness of the Spirit (Luke 3:22; 4:1). These religious activities were done earnestly (Heb. 5:7) and habitually (Luke 4:16) as the means of a truly human spiritual growth process.

Given Jesus's divine nature, the normality of most of his earthly life is staggering. It seems that Jesus spent the first thirty years of his life looking rather ordinary, in relative obscurity, doing manual labor, taking care of his family, and being faithful to whatever his Father called him to do. In his public ministry Jesus performed miraculous signs and delivered authoritative teaching that could only come from God, and this was shockingly offensive for the people of his hometown, who saw Jesus's simplicity and humility as incompatible with messianic wisdom and power:

> Coming to his hometown he taught them in their synagogue, so that they were astonished, and said, "Where did this man get this wisdom and these mighty works? Is not this the carpenter's son? Is not his mother called Mary? And are not his brothers James and Joseph and Simon and Judas? And are not all his sisters with us? Where then did this man get all these things?" And they took offense at him. But Jesus said to them, "A prophet is not without honor except in his hometown and in his own household." (Matt. 13:54–57)

Jesus did not cease to be fully human after the resurrection. He will be a man forever as he represents redeemed humanity for all of eternity (Acts 1:11; 9:5; 1 Cor. 9:1; 15:8; 1 Tim. 2:5; Heb. 7:25; Rev. 1:13).

Implications of the Humanity of Christ

Humans have been sinful ever since the fall. Therefore, it is easy to assume that being sinful is an essential, necessary part of being a "human being." But this is not true. Jesus was human and yet did not sin. In becoming a man, Jesus *reveals the nature of true humanity*. His humanity gives a glimpse of what our humanity would be, were it not tainted with sin. He shows that the problem with humanity is not that we are humans, but rather that we are *fallen*. Jesus's human nature shows the potential of humanity as God intended. This display of sinless humanity reaffirms God's declaration that creation in all its original dimensions (material and spiritual), including humanity, is by divine definition *very* good (Gen. 1:31).

1. Jesus's humanity enables *his representative obedience* for us: "Therefore, as one trespass led to condemnation for all men, so one act of righteousness leads to justification and life for all men. For as by the one man's disobedience the many were made sinners, so by the one man's obedience the many will be made righteous" (Rom. 5:18–19). Because Jesus is truly human, his perfect life of obedience and overcoming all temptations— culminating in his perfect substitutionary death—can take the place of human rebellion and failure.

2. Because of Jesus's humanity, he can truly be a *substitutionary sacrifice* for mankind: "Therefore he had to be made like his brothers in every respect, so that he might become a merciful and faithful high priest in the service of God, to make propitiation for the sins of the people" (Heb. 2:17). It was a man who died on the cross when Jesus died, and his death truly atones for the sin of human beings, whose nature he shares.

3. Jesus's humanity makes him the only *effective mediator* between God and man: "For there is one God, and there is one mediator between God and men, the man Christ Jesus" (1 Tim. 2:5). Jesus's divine and human natures enable him to stand in the gap between fallen humans and a holy God.

4. Jesus's humanity enabled him to become a *sympathetic high priest* who experientially understands the difficult plight of humanity in a fallen world: "For we do not have a high priest who is unable to sympathize with our weaknesses, but one who in every respect has been tempted as we are, yet without sin. Let us then with confidence draw near to the throne of grace, that we may receive mercy and find grace to help in time of need" (Heb. 4:15–16; see Heb. 2:18).

5. Jesus's humanity means he is a *true example* and pattern for human character and conduct: "For to this you have been called, because Christ also suffered for you, leaving you an example, so that you might follow in his steps" (1 Pet. 2:21; see

1 John 2:6). Because Jesus's righteous life was accomplished as a human who used the spiritual resources available to all believers (prayer, Scripture, worship, fellowship, the Holy Spirit), his example is one that should truly motivate and encourage us.

Historical Misunderstandings of the Humanity of Christ

A second-century heresy called Docetism denied the true humanity of Christ. Docetism (from the Greek verb *dokeō*, "to seem, to appear to be") was based on the presuppositions of Gnosticism, which held to a radical dichotomy between the physical and spiritual realms and which viewed the physical order as either evil or worthless. These beliefs led to denying any real physical substance to Jesus's humanity. Docetic christology taught that Jesus's physical humanity was just an illusion; one of Docetism's statements was that "when Jesus walked on the beach, he left no footprints." This heresy has devastating effects on the correct view of Christ, salvation, revelation, and creation. In this view, Christ does not represent humanity in his atoning work, nor does he show us God in human form. It also erodes a biblically positive view of creation, which leads to either a negative or an indifferent perspective on life in the body. The New Testament refutes the seeds of what later became Gnosticism, with its docetic view of Christ. John strongly condemns any view that denies Christ's full, physical humanity: "By this you know the Spirit of God: every spirit that confesses that *Jesus Christ has come in the flesh* is from God, and every spirit that does not confess Jesus is not from God. This is the spirit of the antichrist, which you heard was coming and now is in the world already" (1 John 4:2–3).

Apollinarianism was another early heresy that denied Christ's full humanity. Apollinarius (fourth century AD) believed humans had bodies, animal souls, and rational spirits. He thought the divine *logos* in Christ took the place of the rational spirit of a human. This view was successfully opposed in the fourth century by Gregory of Nazianzus and Athanasius, and was rejected at the Council of Constantinople in AD 381. The council showed that if Jesus is only, as it were, two-thirds human, full redemption of fully human people is lost. Gregory's famous quotation was: "That which He has not assumed He has not healed; but that which is united to His Godhead is also saved." Jesus had to assume every element in a human nature in order to fully redeem humanity.

These two heresies teach believers to appreciate the importance of the humanity of Christ as well as provide a lesson on theological method. Both of these views bring presuppositions about humanity to the Bible and conform biblical teaching to them, rather than allowing Scripture to dictate everything, including presuppositions. Theological method must always allow the teaching of Scripture to shape theological conclusions rather than transform its teaching on the basis of alien assumptions. Countless theological errors have occurred by imposing human ideas on the Bible.

THE DISTINCTION AND UNITY OF CHRIST'S TWO NATURES

Along with Jesus's full deity and humanity, the third and fourth necessary affirmations of biblical christology are that in the incarnation, the divine and human natures remain *distinct*, and the natures are completely *united* in one person. The best evidence of these two realities are passages of Scripture where Jesus's divine glory and human humility are brought together:

> For to us a child is born,
>   to us a son is given;
> and the government shall be upon his shoulder,
>   and his name shall be called
> Wonderful Counselor, *Mighty God*,
>   Everlasting Father, Prince of Peace. (Isa. 9:6)

> For unto you is *born* this day in the city of David a Savior, who is Christ the *Lord*. (Luke 2:11)

> And the Word became *flesh* and dwelt among us, and we have seen his *glory*, glory as of the only Son from the Father, full of grace and truth. (John 1:14)

> Concerning his Son, who was *descended from David according to the flesh* and was declared to be the *Son of God* in power *according to the Spirit of holiness* by his resurrection from the dead, Jesus Christ our Lord. (Rom. 1:3–4)

> None of the rulers of this age understood this, for if they had, they would not have *crucified* the *Lord of glory*. (1 Cor. 2:8)

> But when the fullness of time had come, *God sent forth his Son, born of woman*, born under the law, to redeem those who were under the law, so that we might receive adoption as sons. (Gal. 4:4–5)

These verses present the profound mystery of the eternal, infinite Son of God stepping into time and space and taking on a human nature. There is no greater thought that we could ever ponder.

Implications of the Two Natures of Christ

The belief that Jesus is one person with both divine and human natures has great significance for the possibility of fallen people entering into a relationship with God. Christ must *be* both God and man if he is to mediate *between* God and man, make atonement for sin, and be a sympathetic high priest:

> For in him *all the fullness of God* was pleased to dwell, and through him *to reconcile* to himself all things, whether

on earth or in heaven, *making peace by the blood of his cross.* (Col. 1:19–20)

For there is one God, and there is *one mediator between God and men*, the man Christ Jesus. (1 Tim. 2:5)

Therefore he *had to be made like his brothers in every respect*, so that he might become a merciful and faithful high priest in the service of God, to *make propitiation* for the sins of the people. (Heb. 2:17)

In his seminal work *Why God Became Man*, Anselm of Canterbury (c. AD 1033–1109) summarized the importance of the two natures of Christ for his atoning work by saying, "It is necessary that the self-same Person who is to make this satisfaction [for humanity's sins] be perfect God and perfect man, since He *cannot* make it unless He be really God, and He *ought not* to make it unless He be really man."[1]

HISTORICAL MISUNDERSTANDINGS OF THE UNITY OF CHRIST'S NATURES

Figure 8.1 lists six historical heresies related to the person of Christ. The first four heresies are explained above. *Nestorianism* pressed the distinction between the natures of Christ so much that Christ was made to appear as two persons in one body. *Eutychianism* stressed the unity of the natures to the point where any distinction between them was lost, and Christ was thought to be some new entity, with only one nature, greater than mere man while being fully God in a novel way.

---

[1]Anselm of Canterbury, *Why God Became Man*, bk. 2, ch. 7.

Fig. 8.1

HERESIES CONCERNING THE PERSON OF CHRIST

Ebionism	denies the deity of Christ
Arianism	denies the fullness of the deity of Christ
Docetism	denies the humanity of Christ
Apollinarianism	denies the fullness of the humanity of Christ
Nestorianism	denies the unity of the natures in one person
Eutychianism	denies the distinction of the natures

In AD 451, leaders of the church assembled at Chalcedon (outside of ancient Constantinople) and wrote a creed affirming both Jesus's full humanity and his full deity, with his two natures united in one person. Thereby all six christological heresies were rejected. This creed, formulated at Chalcedon, became the church's foundational statement on Christ. The Chalcedonian Creed reads as follows:

> We, then, following the holy Fathers, all with one consent, teach men to confess one and the same Son, our Lord Jesus Christ, the same perfect in Godhead and also perfect in manhood; truly God and truly man, of a reasonable soul and body; consubstantial with the Father according to the Godhead, and consubstantial with us according to the Manhood; in all things like unto us, without sin; begotten before all ages of the Father according to the Godhead, and in these latter days, for us and for our salvation, born of the Virgin Mary, the Mother of God, according to the Manhood; one and the same Christ, Son, Lord, Only-begotten, *to be acknowledged in two natures, inconfusedly, unchangeably, indivisibly, inseparably; the distinction of natures being by no means taken away by the union, but rather the property of each nature being preserved, and concurring in one Person and one Subsistence,* not parted or divided into two persons, but one and the same Son,

and only begotten, God the Word, the Lord Jesus Christ,
as the prophets from the beginning have declared concerning him, and the Lord Jesus Christ himself has taught us,
and the Creed of the holy Fathers has handed down to us.
(Emphasis added)

Implications of Chalcedonian Christology

The Chalcedonian Creed teaches the church how to talk about
the two natures of Christ without falling into error. In particular,
Chalcedon teaches the church to affirm that:

1. One nature of Christ is sometimes seen doing things in
which his other nature does not share.

2. Anything that either nature does, the person of Christ
does. He, God incarnate, is the active agent every time.

3. The incarnation is a matter of Christ's *gaining* human
attributes, not of his *giving up* divine attributes. He gave up the
glory of divine life (2 Cor. 8:9; Phil. 2:6), but not the possession
of divine powers.

4. We must look first to the Gospel accounts of Jesus
Christ's ministry in order to see the incarnation actualized, rather
than follow fanciful speculations shaped by erroneous human
assumptions.

5. The initiative for the incarnation came from God, not
from man.

While this creed does not solve all questions about the mystery of the incarnation, it has been accepted by Roman Catho-
lic, Orthodox, and Protestant churches throughout history, and
it has never needed any major alteration because it effectively
articulates the biblical tension of Christ's two natures, completely
united in one person.

SCRIPTURE MEMORY AND MEDITATION

"For in him all the fullness of God was pleased to dwell, and through him to reconcile to himself all things, whether on earth or in heaven, making peace by the blood of his cross." (Col. 1:19–20)

Questions for Application and Discussion

1. How should Jesus's deity influence the way you think about worshiping and obeying him?

2. How does the deity of Christ that is clearly taught in the Bible help to explain why he said he was the only way to God? If he was only a great moral teacher, how are we to understand his claims to be God?

3. How has your understanding of the full humanity of Christ changed after reading this chapter? How does his full humanity increase your confidence in him as your representative in his life, death, and resurrection?

4. How does the fact that God became a man enhance your appreciation for humanity and physical reality?

5. Do you think you have neglected the implications of Christ's deity or humanity? How does a biblical understanding of the person of Christ affect how you think about portrayals of Christ in contemporary culture?

For Further Study

Bruce, F. F. *Jesus, Lord & Savior*. The Jesus Library. Downers Grove, IL: InterVarsity Press, 1986.

Dawson, Gerrit Scott. *Jesus Ascended: The Meaning of Christ's Continuing Incarnation*. Phillipsburg, NJ: P&R, 2004.

Erickson, Millard. *The Word Became Flesh: A Contemporary Incarnational Christology*. Grand Rapids, MI: Baker, 1991.

Harris, Murray J. *Jesus as God*. Grand Rapids, MI: Baker, 1992.

Macleod, Donald. *The Person of Christ*. Contours of Christian Theology. Downers Grove, IL: InterVarsity Press, 1998.

Marshall, I. Howard. *I Believe in the Historical Jesus*. Grand Rapids, MI: Eerdmans, 1977.

McGrath, Alister E. *Understanding Jesus: Who He Is and Why He Matters*. Grand Rapids, MI: Zondervan, 1987.

Reymond, Robert L. *Jesus, Divine Messiah*. Phillipsburg, NJ: Presbyterian and Reformed, 1990.

Sproul, R. C. *The Glory of Christ*. Wheaton, IL: Tyndale, 1990.

Walvoord, John F. *Jesus Christ Our Lord*. Chicago: Moody, 1969.

Wells, David F. *The Person of Christ: A Biblical and Historical Analysis of the Incarnation*. Westchester, IL: Crossway, 1984.

9

WHO IS THE HOLY SPIRIT?

"The work of the Spirit is to impart life, to implant hope, to give liberty, to testify of Christ, to guide us into all truth, to teach us all things, to comfort the believer, and to convict the world of sin." —Dwight L. Moody

The Holy Spirit is a fully and completely divine person who possesses all of the divine attributes. God the Spirit applies the work of God the Son. The Spirit's distinct role is to accomplish the unified will of the Father and the Son and to be in personal relationship with both of them.

THE PERSONHOOD OF THE HOLY SPIRIT

The Holy Spirit is a distinct personal being with definite characteristics. He is not merely an impersonal force or an emanation of the power of God. (See the discussion of modalism in chapter 7.)

The baptismal perspective of Matthew 28:19–20, "baptizing them in [or into] the name [singular] of the Father and of the

Son and of the Holy Spirit," puts the Spirit on an equal plane with the Father and the Son in his deity and personhood (see also Matt. 3:13–17; Rom. 8:9; 1 Cor. 12:4–6; 2 Cor. 13:14; Eph. 4:4–6; 1 Pet. 1:2).

The personal nature of the Holy Spirit is evident in his title "Comforter" or "Helper" (Greek, *Paraklētos*) found in John 12:26; 14:16, 26; 15:26; and 16:7. Jesus says he will send the Comforter, who will take his place as his disciples' helper: "Nevertheless, I tell you the truth: it is to your advantage that I go away, for if I do not go away, the Helper will not come to you. But if I go, I will send him to you" (John 16:7). An impersonal force could never provide comfort as Jesus did. The Holy Spirit must be personal in order to fulfill this most personal ministry.

Scripture speaks of several activities of the Spirit (see fig. 9.1) that can be performed only if he is a personal agent. All of these activities of the Holy Spirit are profoundly personal, and they interrelate with the Father and Son in a way that could only be through the Spirit's distinct personal nature.

Fig. 9.1

PERSONAL ACTIONS OF THE HOLY SPIRIT

The Spirit comforts.	John 12:26; 14:16, 26; 15:26; 16:7
The Spirit teaches.	John 14:26; 1 Cor. 2:13
The Spirit speaks.	Acts 8:29; 13:2
The Spirit makes decisions.	Acts 15:28
The Spirit grieves over sin.	Eph. 4:30
The Spirit overrules human actions.	Acts 16:6–7
The Spirit searches the deep things of God and knows the thoughts of God.	1 Cor. 2:10–11
The Spirit determines the distribution of spiritual gifts.	1 Cor. 12:11

The Spirit interprets and brings human prayer before the throne of the Father.	Rom. 8:26–27
The Spirit assures believers of their adoption.	Rom. 8:16
The Spirit bears witness to and glorifies Christ.	John 15:26; 16:14

THE DEITY OF THE HOLY SPIRIT

The Holy Spirit possesses all the divine attributes without limit, as shown in figure 9.2. When the Holy Spirit works, it is God who is working. Jesus taught that regeneration is the work of God: "Truly, truly, I say to you, unless one is born of water and the Spirit, he cannot enter the kingdom of God" (John 3:5). The divine agent that brings this rebirth is the Spirit: "The wind blows where it wishes, and you hear its sound, but you do not know where it comes from or where it goes. So it is with everyone who is born of the Spirit" (John 3:8). God's speaking through the prophets is accomplished through the work of the Spirit. As Paul says in Acts 28:25–26, "The Holy Spirit was right in saying to your fathers through Isaiah the prophet: 'Go to this people, and say, You will indeed hear but never understand, and you will indeed see but never perceive.'" This is a quotation from Isaiah 6:9–10, which is an address from Yahweh to Isaiah. Here in Acts 28:25–26, Paul attributes the words to the Holy Spirit.

Fig. 9.2

DIVINE ATTRIBUTES OF THE HOLY SPIRIT

The Holy Spirit is eternal.	Heb. 9:14
The Holy Spirit is omnipresent.	Ps. 139:7–10
The Holy Spirit is omniscient.	1 Cor. 2:10–11
The Holy Spirit is omnipotent.	Luke 1:35–37
The Holy Spirit is holy.	Rom. 1:4

Furthermore, the Bible equates a believer's relationship to the Spirit and his relationship with God. To lie to the Spirit is to lie to God: "But Peter said, 'Ananias, why has Satan filled your heart to *lie to the Holy Spirit* and to keep back for yourself part of the proceeds of the land? While it remained unsold, did it not remain your own? And after it was sold, was it not at your disposal? Why is it that you have contrived this deed in your heart? *You have not lied to men but to God*'" (Acts 5:3–4). The Holy Spirit is the one who guarantees God's redeeming work in the lives of believers, and he is the one directly grieved by their sin: "Do not grieve the Holy Spirit of God, by whom you were sealed for the day of redemption" (Eph. 4:30).

THE WORK OF THE HOLY SPIRIT

The Father, Son, and Holy Spirit are equal in nature but distinct in role and relationship. The distinct roles typically have the Father willing, the Son accomplishing, and the Spirit applying the work of the Son. The Spirit is clearly at work in the key events throughout the history of salvation, including creation, Christ's incarnation, Christ's resurrection, human regeneration, the inspiration and illumination of Scripture, and the believer's sanctification.

The Spirit's Role in the Ministry of Jesus

The Spirit's role in the human life of the incarnate Christ is often underappreciated. The Spirit brings about the incarnation (Luke 1:35), anoints Jesus for his public ministry at his baptism (Matt. 3:16; Mark 1:10; Luke 3:21–22), fills Jesus (Luke 4:1), leads and empowers Jesus throughout his earthly life (Luke 4:14, 18), and raises Jesus from the dead (Rom. 8:11). The atoning work of Christ is also a Trinitarian accomplishment, with the Spirit playing a prominent role: "how much more will the blood of Christ, who *through the eternal Spirit* offered himself without blemish to God, purify our conscience from dead works to serve the living God" (Heb. 9:14).

The Spirit's Work in God's People

The reality of God's presence is brought to God's people by God's Spirit. His work is central in the promises of new covenant realities. "And it shall come to pass afterward, that I will pour out my Spirit on all flesh; your sons and your daughters shall prophesy, your old men shall dream dreams, and your young men shall see visions" (Joel 2:28); "And I will not hide my face anymore from them, when I pour out my Spirit upon the house of Israel, declares the Lord GOD" (Ezek. 39:29). These promises are inaugurated at Pentecost when the Spirit's power is poured out on all nations.

The Spirit is the primary person of the Trinity at work in applying the finished work of Christ in the lives of God's people. The acts of the Holy Spirit—rather than the acts of the apostles—are the focal point of the book of Acts. He is the one who enables the apostles to accomplish all their kingdom-advancing work. The power of the Spirit is the catalyst of spiritual transformation. Prayer, church attendance, moral living, coming from a Christian family, and knowing all the right religious words are not sufficient basis for assurance of one's salvation. But one clear guarantee that someone has passed from death into life is the Spirit's work of transforming that person's manner of living. He marks the life and character of believers in a definitive way, as seen in Ephesians 1:13: "In him you also, when you heard the word of truth, the gospel of your salvation, and believed in him, were sealed with the promised Holy Spirit" (see 2 Cor. 1:21–22).

In the book of Acts, the Spirit's work was often manifested in miraculous gifts such as speaking in tongues and prophesying. While the Spirit may still choose to work in these ways, it is the fruit of the Spirit that is the normative and necessary evidence of God's work in someone's life: "But the fruit of the

Spirit is love, joy, peace, patience, kindness, goodness, faithfulness, gentleness, self-control; against such things there is no law" (Gal. 5:22–23). After the inward renewal that makes someone who has trusted Christ a new creation, the Spirit also brings spiritual understanding, convicts of sin, reveals the truth of the Word, brings assurance of salvation, empowers for holy living, teaches, and comforts.

Although the Holy Spirit's work is evident in the life of someone who is truly born again, even believers can operate "in the flesh" (i.e., by their own self and natural ability apart from God), rather than by Spirit-empowered transformation. God is pleased when his people walk in the Spirit and thus show evidence of his work. God-honoring, unified Christian community is possible only when believers walk in the Spirit. This is why Christians are reminded to "walk in a manner worthy of the calling to which you have been called, with all humility and gentleness, with patience, bearing with one another in love, eager to maintain *the unity of the Spirit* in the bond of peace" (Eph. 4:1–3).

The Holy Spirit Glorifies Christ

The Holy Spirit's work can easily be overlooked. Perhaps one reason for this is that one of his primary roles is to glorify Christ by testifying to his kingdom and his saving work, past, present, and future: "When the Spirit of truth comes, he will guide you into all the truth, for he will not speak on his own authority, but whatever he hears he will speak, and he will declare to you the things that are to come. *He will glorify me*, for he will take what is mine and declare it to you" (John 16:13–14). Because the Holy Spirit's purpose is to glorify Christ, he is honored and takes delight when this objective is accomplished. Jesus is the focus of the Spirit's ministry, and believers honor the Spirit by depending on his help in order to honor Christ. The Holy Spirit works to advance the work of Christ to the glory of the Father, and he empowers and anoints the people of God to do the same.

As seen in figure 9.3, the Holy Spirit glorifies Christ in four fundamental ways. The Spirit continually points to the beauty and wonder of the Son so that people will be drawn to him, become like him, and point others to him as well: "And we all, with unveiled face, beholding the glory of the Lord, are being transformed into the same image from one degree of glory to another. For this comes from the Lord who is the Spirit" (2 Cor. 3:18).

Fig. 9.3

HOW THE HOLY SPIRIT GLORIFIES CHRIST TODAY

The Spirit illumines the Bible (the centrality of Christ).	Luke 24:27, 44–48
The Spirit empowers gospel preaching (proclamation of Christ).	Acts 1:8
The Spirit brings regeneration (new life in Christ).	John 3:5–8
The Spirit sanctifies the believer (transformation into the image of Christ).	Rom. 8:29; 1 John 3:2

Humans become like what they adore. The Spirit works to foster adoration of Christ so that people will become like him. Thus, sanctification flows from adoration, and both are accomplished by the Spirit in the believer's life.

Implications of the Spirit's Work

The ultimate goal of all of life is to know and love God, make him known, and thereby glorify him. This goal is accomplished primarily through the work of the Holy Spirit. Reading the Bible, going to church, Christian fellowship, spiritual disciplines, service, and worship are merely ways of playing at religion if all of these activities are not empowered, guided, and filled by the

Spirit. If he is not present, even these good things are fleshly, empty, and repugnant to God: "For if you live according to the flesh you will die, but if by the Spirit you put to death the deeds of the body, you will live" (Rom. 8:13). A life pleasing to God involves daily dependence on the precious Holy Spirit. He is to be known, sought, and loved. His awakening and empowering have always been the essential ingredients of true and lasting works of God in the lives of his people. His work in the transformed lives of believers is the key to a Christian life that experiences God's blessing and becomes an effective witness to a cynical, skeptical world. Because of the Spirit's presence, true Christians are no longer slaves to sin: "You, however, are not in the flesh but in the Spirit, if in fact the Spirit of God dwells in you. Anyone who does not have the Spirit of Christ does not belong to him" (Rom. 8:9).

We tend to attribute Jesus's holiness and power in ministry to his divine nature rather than to the work of the Holy Spirit in his human life. As a result, believers may discount Jesus as their true example. In his holy living and powerful ministry, Jesus normally drew from the same resources that are available to all believers, especially the leading and empowering of the Holy Spirit.

The three persons of the Trinity have now been revealed in redemptive history, and the Holy Spirit is bringing their work to a magnificent consummation. Many believers expect a world revival in the last days that will include all peoples. Even if such a revival does not come in the generation that is now alive, God's people should be giving glimpses of that coming revival in the character of their lives even today. Such glimpses contribute to fulfilling the Great Commission. Jesus sent his followers even as the Father sent him (John 20:21), and living under and in that authority they are able to say with Jesus, "The Spirit of the Lord is upon me, because he has anointed me to preach good news to the poor. He has sent me to proclaim liberty to the captives . . ." (Luke 4:18). When the Spirit works, the gospel will be boldly proclaimed and God's kingdom will advance.

SCRIPTURE MEMORY AND MEDITATION

"But you will receive power when the Holy Spirit has come upon you, and you will be my witnesses in Jerusalem and in all Judea and Samaria, and to the end of the earth." (Acts 1:8)

Questions for Application and Discussion

1. Have you neglected the person and work of the Holy Spirit in your understanding of the Christian life? How should the personhood of the Spirit shape the way you relate to him? How conscious are you that your growth as a Christian depends on the Spirit?

2. How do you think you should relate to the Holy Spirit differently than you do to the Father and the Son? How should you relate to him in the same way as you relate to the Father and Son?

3. Have you ever had an experience when it was obvious that the Holy Spirit was at work? If so, what was it that made his power or presence obvious? What could you do to become more dependent on the work of the Spirit in your life?

4. How can you tell the difference between doing something "in the flesh" as opposed to "in the Spirit"?

5. Jesus said that it was better for his followers if he left and the Spirit came instead (John 16:7). Is it hard for you to believe this? If so, why do you think we would

prefer to have Christ in the flesh with us rather than the Spirit? What reasons can you think of that would make it advantageous for the Spirit to be here rather than Christ in the flesh during this period of history?

For Further Study

Carson, D. A. *Showing the Spirit: A Theological Exposition of 1 Corinthians 12–14*. Grand Rapids, MI: Baker, 1987.

Cole, Graham. *Engaging with the Holy Spirit: Real Questions, Practical Answers*. Wheaton, IL: Crossway, 2008.

_____. *He Who Gives Life: The Doctrine of the Holy Spirit*. Wheaton, IL: Crossway, 2007.

Ferguson, Sinclair B. *The Holy Spirit*. Contours of Christian Theology. Downers Grove, IL: InterVarsity Press, 1997.

Green, Michael. *I Believe in the Holy Spirit*. Grand Rapids, MI: Eerdmans, 1975.

Hawthorne, Gerald. *The Presence and the Power: The Significance of the Holy Spirit in the Life and Ministry of Jesus*. Dallas: Word, 1991.

Packer, J. I. *Keep in Step with the Spirit*. Old Tappan, NJ: Revell, 1984.

Sproul, R. C. *The Mystery of the Holy Spirit*. Wheaton, IL: Tyndale, 1990.

Stott, John R. W. *Baptism and Fullness: The Work of the Holy Spirit Today*. Downers Grove, IL: InterVarsity Press, 1964.

10

WHAT DID JESUS CHRIST ACCOMPLISH?

"We rest our souls on a finished work, if we rest them on the work of Jesus Christ the Lord. We need not fear that either sin, or Satan, or law shall condemn us at the last day. We may lean back on the thought, that we have a Savior who has done all, paid all, accomplished all, performed all that is necessary for our salvation."
—J. C. Ryle

Why did God become a man in Jesus Christ? He came to restore what was lost in the fall of humanity and take back the world he made. The doctrine of the work of Christ is traditionally organized by the *offices* he fulfilled and the *stages* of his work.

111

THE OFFICES OF CHRIST

Christ perfectly fulfilled the Old Testament offices of *prophet*, *priest*, and *king*. These offices or roles in the Old Testament reveal aspects of God's word, presence, and power. The anointing and empowering of the Holy Spirit and the favor of God were essential if these offices were to truly represent God. Old Testament prophets, priests, and kings foreshadowed the Messiah who would one day ultimately and definitively be manifest as God's Son and Word, bringing access to God's presence and inaugurating the kingdom of God.

The Prophetic Work of Christ

A true prophet of God proclaims God's word to people. God promised Moses that he would raise up a messianic prophet who would authoritatively speak for God: "I will raise up for them a prophet like you from among their brothers. And I will put my words in his mouth, and he shall speak to them all that I command him. And whoever will not listen to my words that he shall speak in my name, I myself will require it of him" (Deut. 18:18–19). Those in Jesus's day expected the Messiah to fulfill the prophetic role the Old Testament foretold. As the author of Hebrews tells us, Jesus's prophetic ministry brought all that the previous prophets of God had proclaimed to a definitive culmination: "Long ago, at many times and in many ways, God spoke to our fathers by the prophets, but *in these last days* he has spoken to us by his Son, whom he appointed the heir of all things, through whom also he created the world" (Heb. 1:1–2). Jesus equated his own words with the authoritative words of the Hebrew Scriptures, showing that he knew his words were the very words of God. He recognized the unchanging authority of the Mosaic law (Matt. 5:18) and gave his teaching the same weight: "Heaven and earth will pass away, but *my words* will not pass away" (Matt. 24:35). Because Jesus's words are the very words of God, they are divinely authoritative, eternal, and unchangeable.

Jesus's prophetic authority is vastly superior to that of any other prophet because he speaks God's words *as* God. The divine authority of his words is based on his identity as God incarnate. He proclaimed God's truth as the One who is the truth (John 14:6). His word is the ultimate Word.

Implications of the Prophetic Office of Christ. Since Jesus Christ is the true and perfect prophet, he is the ultimate source of truth about God, ourselves, the meaning of life, the future, right and wrong, salvation, and heaven and hell. The voice of Jesus in the Word of God should be eagerly sought and obeyed without reservation or delay. Even though Jesus perfectly fulfills the office of prophet, God's plan is for the church to represent him with its own ongoing prophetic voice, proclaiming truth into the world. Paul certainly saw his own ministry as speaking for God: "Therefore, we are ambassadors for Christ, God making his appeal through us. We implore you on behalf of Christ, be reconciled to God" (2 Cor. 5:20).

The Priestly Work of Christ

While a prophet speaks God's words to the people, a priest represents the people before God and represents God before the people. He is a man who stands in the presence of God as a mediator (Heb. 5:1). The priestly work of Christ involves both *atonement* and *intercession*.

The Atonement of Christ. The atonement is central to God's work in the history of salvation (Mark 10:45; 1 Cor. 2:2; 15:3). Atonement is the making of enemies into friends by averting the punishment that their sin would otherwise incur. Sinners in rebellion against God need a representative to offer sacrifice on their behalf if they are to be reconciled to God. Jesus's righteous life and atoning death on behalf of sinners is the only way for fallen man to be restored into right relationship with a holy God.

Even with the extensive requirements for the priesthood in the Old Testament, there was a realization that these human priests were unable to make lasting atonement (Ps. 110:1, 4; see Heb. 10:1–4). Jesus alone was able to make an offering sufficient for the eternal forgiveness of sins. Because Jesus was without sin, he was uniquely able to offer sacrifice without needing atonement for himself. In offering himself as the perfect, spotless Lamb of God, he could actually pay for sins in a way that Old Testament sacrifices could not. Jesus's atoning offering was thus eternal, complete, and once-for-all. No other sacrifice will ever be needed to pay the price for human sin.

The Necessity of the Atonement. Jesus died because of human sin, but also in accordance with God's plan. The reality of human sin is vividly seen in the envy of the Jewish leaders (Matt. 27:18), Judas's greed (Matt. 26:14–16), and Pilate's cowardice (Matt. 27:26). However, Jesus gave his life of his own initiative and courageous love: "I am the good shepherd. The good shepherd lays down his life for the sheep. . . . For this reason the Father loves me, because I lay down my life that I may take it up again. No one takes it from me, but I lay it down of my own accord. I have authority to lay it down, and I have authority to take it up again. This charge I have received from my Father" (John 10:11, 17–18; see Gal. 2:20).

The Father's divine initiative also led to Jesus's atoning work: "He who did not spare his own Son but gave him up for us all, how will he not also with him graciously give us all things?" (Rom. 8:32; see Isa. 53:6, 10; John 3:16). As in all events of human history, God's sovereign determination works in a way that is compatible with human decisions and actions. Even human sin is woven into God's divine purposes, as we see in verses that say Jesus was "delivered up according to the definite plan and foreknowledge of God . . ." (Acts 2:23), and that "Herod and Pontius Pilate, along with the Gentiles and the peoples of Israel" were gathered together to do "whatever [God's] hand and [God's] plan had predestined to take place" (Acts 4:27–28).

Christ came to save sinners in order to accomplish God's will. Christ died in accordance with God's sovereign, free, gracious choice—not because he was in any way compelled to offer salvation to mankind because of something inherent in us. God did not save fallen angels (2 Pet. 2:4), and he would have been entirely justified in condemning all of fallen humanity to hell; it is only because of his amazing mercy and grace that anyone can be saved.

The Bible explains atonement using numerous metaphors and images. Figure 10.1 shows the varied images the Bible uses to describe the achievement that is at the heart of the gospel.

Fig. 10.1

BIBLICAL DESCRIPTIONS OF THE ATONEMENT

Type of Language	Biblical Words	Human Need	The Result
Language of Old Testament sacrifices	Blood, lamb, sacrifice	We are guilty.	We are forgiven.
Language of personal relationships	Reconciliation	We are alienated from God.	We are brought back into intimate fellowship with God.
Language of righteous anger at wrongdoing	Propitiation	We are under God's holy wrath.	God's wrath is satisfied/quenched.
Language of the marketplace	Redemption, ransom	We are enslaved.	We are set free.

Type of Language	Biblical Words	Human Need	The Result
Language of the law court	Justification	We are condemned.	We are pardoned and counted as righteous.
Language of the battlefield	Victory, deliverance, rescue	We are facing dreadful enemies.	We are delivered and are triumphant in Christ.

Throughout church history, various aspects of the atonement have garnered particular attention. For instance, at different times theologians have stressed the *ransom* imagery, the selfless *example* of Christ, and the *victory* of Christ over evil. These aspects of the atonement, rightly understood, contain true and important insights, but the crux of the atonement is Christ taking the place of sinners and enduring the wrath of God as their substitute sacrifice. This is evident in passages like 2 Corinthians 5:21 ("For our sake he made him to be sin who knew no sin, so that in him we might become the righteousness of God") and Isaiah 53:4–5 ("Surely he has borne our griefs and carried our sorrows; yet we esteemed him stricken, smitten by God, and afflicted. But he was wounded for our transgressions; he was crushed for our iniquities; upon him was the chastisement that brought us peace, and with his stripes we are healed"; see Rom. 3:25; Heb. 2:17; 1 John 2:2; 4:10). The fundamental problem of human sin has been solved in Christ's dying for sinners who deserved eternal judgment. Any attempt to diminish the importance of the penal substitution of Christ for us (i.e., the truth that Christ died to pay the *penalty* for our sins) will diminish God's holiness and wrath, as well as the heinous depth of human sin.

Christ's physical suffering on the cross was outweighed by the emotional, psychological, and spiritual anguish of bearing the sin of mankind and having the wrath of the Father poured out on him. The abandonment and bearing of God's wrath that

Jesus experienced on the cross is beyond our comprehension. On account of this merciful, substitutionary sacrifice he will be worshiped for all eternity by those who are his (Rev. 5:11–12). While Jesus's death for sinners was the basis of his atoning work, his life of perfect righteousness in their place was also necessary to win their forgiveness. He not only *died* for rebels, he also *lived* for them (Rom. 5:19; 2 Cor. 5:21; Phil. 3:8–9).

The Intercession of Christ. Jesus's priestly work on the cross atoned for sin once for all. Grounded in that atoning work, his priestly work of intercession continues now and forevermore on behalf of his people: "Who is to condemn? Christ Jesus is the one who died—more than that, who was raised—who is at the right hand of God, who indeed is interceding for us" (Rom. 8:34); Christ "is able to save to the uttermost those who draw near to God through him, since he always lives to make intercession for them" (Heb. 7:25). Jesus is alive and always at work representing and bringing requests for believers before the throne of God, interceding in heaven for them. He is the God-man who mediates and represents fallen people based on his fully sufficient work on the cross, and his intervention never fails. Jesus, the sinner's divine lawyer, never loses a case: "My little children, I am writing these things to you so that you may not sin. But if anyone does sin, we have an advocate with the Father, Jesus Christ the righteous" (1 John 2:1).

As the people who constitute the church are intended to have a prophetic voice as Christ's ambassadors, God also intends to use the church in a priestly role to usher people into his presence. Because of Christ's work, all of God's people are viewed as priests with priestly access into his presence and with the privilege of representing people before God (1 Pet. 2:9; Rev. 5:9–10). Prayer, preaching, gospel proclamation, and taking initiative in personal, spiritual ministry are all ways in which God's people can encourage others to seek and know God, and can thereby fulfill their call to represent Christ as a kingdom of priests.

The Kingly Work of Christ

Christ is not only the ultimate prophet and priest, he is also the divine king. Unlike the kings of Israel who were intended to foreshadow the Messiah, Jesus's reign as messianic King is in no way limited. He rules over all creation and for all time (Luke 1:31–33; Col. 1:17). This rule most directly touches believers at present, but one day all peoples will bow to his royal authority (Phil. 2:9–10). In addition to his comprehensive rule, Christ the King also defends, protects, and shepherds his people and will one day judge all the world's inhabitants—past, present, and future.

God's people represent their King when they work to see kingdom realities spread in the world. When they seek social justice—fighting to relieve the plight of the poor, disenfranchised, or unborn—they are working to spread the values of their King. When they work hard and live as good citizens, they are salt and light in a dark world, ultimately serving the interest of their King. One day, when Christ makes all things new, those who are his subjects will reign with their King: "The saying is trustworthy, for: If we have died with him, we will also live with him; if we endure, we will also reign with him . . ." (2 Tim. 2:11–12a; see Rev. 5:9–10).

THE STAGES OF CHRIST'S WORK

There is perhaps no more comprehensive yet concise statement on the work of Christ than Philippians 2:5–11:

> Have this mind among yourselves, which is yours in Christ Jesus, who, though he was in the form of God, did not count equality with God a thing to be grasped, but made himself nothing, taking the form of a servant, being born in the likeness of men. And being found in human form, he humbled himself by becoming obedient to the point of death, even death on a cross. Therefore God has highly exalted him and bestowed on him the name that is above every name, so that

at the name of Jesus every knee should bow, in heaven and
on earth and under the earth, and every tongue confess that
Jesus Christ is Lord, to the glory of God the Father.

These verses teach the profound humility and eventual exaltation of Christ in the history of salvation. The key sequence set
out here has been described as the ten stages of Christ's work,
divided into a humiliation phase and an exaltation phase. The
stages are: (1) preincarnate glory; (2) incarnation; (3) earthly life;
(4) crucifixion; (5) resurrection; (6) ascension; (7) sitting at God's
right hand; (8) second coming; (9) future reign (some think this
will be a millennial reign); (10) eternal glory.

The ten stages and two phases can be visualized as shown
in figure 10.2.

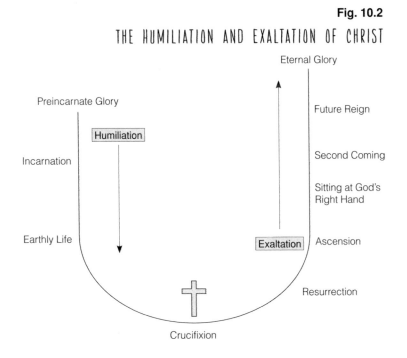

Fig. 10.2

THE HUMILIATION AND EXALTATION OF CHRIST

Eternal Glory

Preincarnate Glory

Future Reign

Humiliation

Incarnation

Second Coming

Sitting at God's
Right Hand

Earthly Life

Exaltation

Ascension

Resurrection

Crucifixion

Christ's work begins with progressive humility, which leads to his glorious exaltation.

Fig. 10.3

THE HUMILIATION OF CHRIST

Incarnation	"And the Word became flesh and dwelt among us, and we have seen his glory, glory as of the only Son from the Father, full of grace and truth." (John 1:14)
Earthly Life	"For even the Son of Man came not to be served but to serve, and to give his life as a ransom for many." (Mark 10:45)
Crucifixion	"And being found in human form, he humbled himself by becoming obedient to the point of death, even death on a cross." (Phil. 2:8)

Fig. 10.4

THE EXALTATION OF CHRIST

Resurrection	"Jesus said to her, 'I am the resurrection and the life. Whoever believes in me, though he die, yet shall he live, and everyone who lives and believes in me shall never die. Do you believe this?'" (John 11:25–26)
Ascension	"Men of Galilee, why do you stand looking into heaven? This Jesus, who was taken up from you into heaven, will come in the same way as you saw him go into heaven." (Acts 1:11)
Heavenly Session	"Who is to condemn? Christ Jesus is the one who died—more than that, who was raised—who is at the right hand of God, who indeed is interceding for us." (Rom. 8:34)
Second Coming	"For the Lord himself will descend from heaven with a cry of command, with the voice of an archangel, and with the sound of the trumpet of God. And the dead in Christ will rise first." (1 Thess. 4:16)
Eternal Glory	"And I heard every creature in heaven and on earth and under the earth and in the sea, and all that is in them, saying, 'To him who sits on the throne and to the Lamb be blessing and honor and glory and might forever and ever!'" (Rev. 5:13)

Preincarnate Glory

To truly understand the humility of Christ in becoming a man, we must ponder what he gave up in order to make this possible. While we know very little about the experience of God before this world's creation, we do know that he has always existed as one being, the three persons within his being perfectly relating in mutual love and glorification as Father, Son, and Holy Spirit (John 1:1; 17:5, 24). Along with this intra-Trinitarian glorification, angelic beings (creatures themselves) unceasingly worship the triune God. Jesus consented to surrender this perfect heavenly state so he could represent humanity in his incarnation. When he took the role of a servant and assumed a human nature in addition to his divine nature (Phil. 2:5–11), his divinity was veiled in his humanity. He willingly surrendered the continuous heavenly display and acknowledgment of his glorious divine nature. This amazing humility is taught in 2 Corinthians 8:9: "For you know the grace of our Lord Jesus Christ, that though he was rich, yet for your sake he become poor, so that you by his poverty might become rich." Only when the glories of heaven are finally revealed will what Jesus temporarily gave up in coming to earth as a man be most fully understood. What amazing, loving condescension!

The Humiliation of Christ

Incarnation. In the incarnation (lit., "in flesh") Christ took on a full, complete human nature, including a physical body, so that he could truly represent humanity (Phil. 2:6–8; Heb. 2:17). God the Son chose to come to earth in the most humble way, defying expectation. His contemporaries saw him as the son of a poor couple, born in a small, obscure village, and with nothing in his appearance to attract them to himself (see Isa. 53:2). In the incarnation, God shows in a striking manner that he does not value so much of what society often does.

Earthly Life. Christ's earthly life was one of continual humiliation. He subtly and selectively revealed his divine glory, even keeping it a secret at times (Matt. 9:30; Mark 1:44; 5:43). He radically altered the prevalent conception of the Messiah, combining the Suffering Servant of Isaiah 53 with the glorious Conquering King of Daniel 7. Throughout his life Jesus was poor and at times homeless: "Foxes have holes and birds of the air have nests, but the Son of Man has nowhere to lay his head" (Matt. 8:20). His life was one of great and consistent service for the good of others. The last grand gesture of his life before going to the cross was washing his disciples' feet (John 13:1–17). Although multitudes followed him during his public ministry, he also faced frequent persecution and rejection, at times even in his hometown (Luke 4:28–29). The creatures' rejection of their Creator epitomizes human rebellion. John 1:10–11 describes this tragedy: "He was in the world, and the world was made through him, yet the world did not know him. He came to his own, and his own people did not receive him."

Jesus's earthly life ended with some of his closest friends betraying him (Judas), denying him (Peter), and deserting him (all the disciples, Matt. 26:56). His life was filled with rejection, loneliness, poverty, persecution, hunger, temptation, suffering, and finally death.

Crucifixion. Christ's humiliation reached its greatest depth when he gave his life on a criminal's cross for sinful humanity. The cross stands at the center of human history as God's supreme act of love (1 John 4:10, 17) and the only source of redemption for lost and fallen humanity (Rom. 14:9).

The Exaltation of Christ

Resurrection. While Jesus's life of humiliation represented the life of human beings living in a fallen world, his victorious exaltation represents a pattern that will someday be reproduced (and is partially reproduced already) in those who believe in him. The exaltation of Christ began when he left his grave clothes in an empty tomb. Sin, Satan, and death were decisively defeated when Jesus rose from the dead. Jesus foretold his resurrection (e.g., Mark 8:31; 9:31; 10:34) and then actually did rise from the dead (as is shown by convincing historical evidence, such as the empty tomb, numerous eyewitness accounts, the radical change in the disciples' lives, etc.). In addition to defeating sin and death, the resurrection was the Father's validation of the Son's ministry (Rom. 1:4) and it demonstrates the complete effectiveness of Christ's atoning work (Rom. 4:25).

First Corinthians 15 provides the most comprehensive treatment of the benefits of the resurrection. By explaining what would be lost if Jesus had not risen from the dead, Paul provides abundant reason for hope in the truth of the resurrection because "in fact Christ has been raised from the dead, the firstfruits of those who have fallen asleep" (v. 20). Because Christ rose from the dead, the sins of those who rely on him are forgiven (v. 17), the apostolic preaching is true (v. 15), faith in Christ is true and he can be fully trusted (v. 14), those who follow Christ are to be emulated and their preaching is of great value (v. 19), and those who die in Christ will be raised (v. 18). Because of the resurrection, the Christian has great hope that generates confidence in all circumstances. The resurrection is not merely a doctrine to be affirmed intellectually; it is the resounding affirmation that Jesus reigns over all, and the power that raised him from the dead is the Christian's power for living the Christian life on earth and the assurance of eternal life in heaven.

Ascension. The ascension is Christ's return to heaven from earth (Luke 24:50–51; John 14:2, 12; 16:5, 10, 28; Acts 1:6–11; Eph. 4:8–10; 1 Tim. 3:16; Heb. 4:14; 7:26; 9:24). The incarnation does not cease with Christ's ascension. Jesus lives, now and forever, as true man and true God to mediate between God and man

(1 Tim. 2:5). He will come again as he left, fully God and fully man (Acts 1:11).

Jesus's ascension is a crucial event in his ministry because it explicitly shows his continual humanity and the permanence of his resurrection. The importance of the ascension is seen in the fact that it is taught in all of the essential creeds of the church, beginning with the Apostles' Creed. The ascension guarantees that Jesus will always represent humanity before the throne of God as the mediator, intercessor, and advocate for needy humans. Because of the ascension, we can be sure that Jesus's unique resurrection leads the way for the everlasting resurrection of the redeemed. A human face and nail-scarred hands will greet believers one day in heaven.

Jesus also ascended to prepare a place for his people (John 14:2–3) and to enable the Holy Spirit to come (John 16:7), a situation which he said was more advantageous for the church than if he had stayed on earth (John 14:12, 17).

Sitting at God's Right Hand. The current state of Christ's work is called his "heavenly session," which means that he is seated at the right hand of the Father, actively interceding for and reigning over his kingdom, awaiting his second coming (Acts 2:33–36; Rom. 8:34; Eph. 1:20–22; Col. 3:1; Heb. 1:3, 13; 8:1; 10:12; 12:2; 1 Pet. 3:22; Rev. 3:21; 22:1). The Old Testament foretold this phase of the Messiah's work: "The LORD says to my Lord: 'Sit at my right hand, until I make your enemies your footstool'" (Ps. 110:1). Jesus told of the heavenly session that would precede his return when he referred to the messianic imagery of Daniel 7: "From now on you will see the Son of Man seated at the right hand of Power and coming on the clouds of heaven" (Matt. 26:64). The right hand of God is the symbolic place of power, honor, distinction, and prestige. Jesus "sits" to portray the sufficiency of his saving work on earth; he continues a vital, active ministry as he reigns over all creation.

Jesus's current ministry is a great source of comfort, authority, and encouragement for the believer because it ensures that his ministry as Prophet, Priest, and King continues and will one day be acknowledged by all creation. From his current exalted position Jesus pours out his Spirit on his people: "Being therefore exalted at the right hand of God, and having received from the Father the promise of the Holy Spirit, he has poured out this that you yourselves are seeing and hearing" (Acts 2:33). His precious intercession on behalf of his people takes place at the right hand of the Father so that the believer need never fear condemnation: "Who is to condemn? Christ Jesus is the one who died—more than that, who was raised—who is at the right hand of God, who indeed is interceding for us" (Rom. 8:34).

Second Coming and Future Reign. Biblical interpreters are divided as to whether Jesus's coming will occur in one stage or two (see the last chapter on how it all ends). But all agree that someday Christ will return in great glory and there will be a definitive, comprehensive acknowledgment that he is Lord over all. He will then judge the living and the dead. All people and forces that oppose him will be vanquished, including death itself (Matt. 25:31–46; 1 Cor. 15:24–28; 2 Thess. 1:5–10), "so that at the name of Jesus every knee should bow, in heaven and on earth and under the earth, and every tongue confess that Jesus Christ is Lord, to the glory of God the Father" (Phil. 2:10–11).

Eternal Glory. Prior to the incarnation Jesus was glorious. But by displaying his holy character through his incarnate life, death, and resurrection, he received even greater glory. Jesus's preincarnate glory was taken to a new level when he entered into his eternal glory not only as God but as God-Man. His majesty, mercy, love, holiness, wisdom, and power have been manifested sinlessly in a true man, and for this Jesus will be praised for all eternity. Therefore, the worship of heaven focuses on the work of Christ as the worthy Lamb who was slain:

And they sang a new song, saying,

> "Worthy are you to take the scroll
>   and to open its seals,
> for you were slain, and by your blood you ransomed
>   people for God
> from every tribe and language and people and nation,
> and you have made them a kingdom and priests to
>   our God,
>   and they shall reign on the earth. . . .

Worthy is the Lamb who was slain, to receive power and wealth and wisdom and might and honor and glory and blessing!" (Rev. 5:9–10, 12)

Christ's eternal glory, which he fully shares with the Father and the Holy Spirit, is the supreme goal of all that he did. In redeeming a people for himself, he displayed God's perfections so that he will now receive the glory he deserves. That glory will be displayed and acknowledged around his throne, in the songs of heaven forever!

SCRIPTURE MEMORY AND MEDITATION

"And the Word became flesh and dwelt among us, and we have seen his glory, glory as of the only Son from the Father, full of grace and truth." (John 1:14)

Questions for Application and Discussion

1. What did you learn in this chapter that has helped you better appreciate the death of Christ? When you think

about who it actually was that died on the cross, are you more confident that your sins were really atoned for there?

2. How does the representative obedience of Christ factor into your understanding of Christ's work? Does the thought that Christ obeyed for you make you more confident in your sufficiency in Christ?

3. How does the resurrection of Christ transform the way you think about your body now? What do you look forward to most about having a resurrected body? Why do you think the apostle Paul says that if Christ is not raised from the dead then the Christian faith is in vain (1 Cor. 15:17)?

4. Have you thought much about the ascension of Christ before? How has this chapter helped you to better appreciate the importance of the ascension? Is it encouraging to think about the permanent uniting of divine and human natures in Christ so that he can live forever to intercede for you? The Bible says that if you are a believer, you are seated with Christ in heavenly places (Eph. 2:6). How does this realization alter the way you relate to God?

5. Are there ways you have acted in a prophetic, priestly, or kingly way as you have represented Christ? How could you foster more effective exercise of these roles as you grow in Christ?

For Further Study

Clowney, Edmund P. *The Unfolding Mystery: Discovering Christ in the Old Testament.* Phillipsburg, NJ: Presbyterian and Reformed, 1988.

Craig, William Lane. *The Son Rises: The Historical Evidence for the Resurrection of Jesus.* Chicago: Moody, 1981.

Dawson, Gerrit Scott. *Jesus Ascended: The Meaning of Christ's Continuing Incarnation*. Phillipsburg, NJ: P&R, 2004.

Demarest, Bruce. *The Cross and Salvation: The Doctrine of Salvation*. Wheaton, IL: Crossway, 2006.

Green, Michael. *The Empty Cross of Jesus*. The Jesus Library. Downers Grove, IL: InterVarsity Press, 1984.

Jeffery, Steve, Michael Ovey, and Andrew Sach. *Pierced for Our Transgressions: Rediscovering the Glory of Penal Substitution*. Wheaton, IL: Crossway, 2007.

Ladd, George E. *I Believe in the Resurrection of Jesus*. Grand Rapids, MI: Eerdmans, 1975.

McGrath, Alister E. *What Was God Doing on the Cross?* Grand Rapids, MI: Zondervan, 1993.

Morris, Leon. *The Atonement: Its Meaning and Significance*. Downers Grove, IL: InterVarsity Press, 1983.

Murray, John. *Redemption Accomplished and Applied*. Grand Rapids, MI: Eerdmans, 1955, pp. 9–78.

Packer, J. I., and Mark Dever. *In My Place Condemned He Stood: Celebrating the Glory of the Atonement*. Wheaton, IL: Crossway, 2008.

Stott, John R. W. *The Cross of Christ*. Downers Grove, IL: InterVarsity Press, 1986.

Wenham, John. *The Easter Enigma*. London: Paternoster, 1984.

Wright, N. T. *Surprised by Hope: Rethinking Heaven, the Resurrection, and the Mission of the Church*. New York: HarperOne, 2008.

WHAT IS
A HUMAN BEING?

GOD AS CREATOR

God created human beings and everything else that has ever existed. From the first verse of the Bible (which declares that God created the heavens and the earth) to the last chapters of the Bible (where God brings about a new heaven and earth), God is seen as the praiseworthy source of all that is. Worship is the right response to God's creative and sustaining power. Often in the Bible the praise of God's people arises out of the recognition that God made the heavens and the earth:

> You are the LORD, you alone. You have made heaven, the heaven of heavens, with all their host, the earth and all that is on it, the seas and all that is in them; and you preserve all of them; and the host of heaven worships you. (Neh. 9:6)

> Oh come, let us worship and bow down;
>   let us kneel before the LORD, our Maker! (Ps. 95:6; see
>   Acts 14:15)

God's personal, wise power is clearly seen in creation, especially in humanity:

> For you formed my inward parts;
> you knitted me together in my mother's womb.
> I praise you, for I am fearfully and wonderfully made.
> Wonderful are your works;
> my soul knows it very well.
> My frame was not hidden from you,
> when I was being made in secret,
> intricately woven in the depths of the earth. (Ps. 139:13–15)

The key passage for understanding the nature of mankind is Genesis 1:26–28:

> Then God said, "Let us make man in our image, after our likeness. And let them have dominion over the fish of the sea and over the birds of the heavens and over the livestock and over all the earth and over every creeping thing that creeps on the earth."
>
> So God created man in his own image,
> in the image of God he created him;
> male and female he created them.
>
> And God blessed them. And God said to them, "Be fruitful and multiply and fill the earth and subdue it and have dominion over the fish of the sea and over the birds of the heavens and over every living thing that moves on the earth." (see Gen. 2:7; 5:1–2; 9:6; Matt. 19:4; Acts 17:24–25)

Both men and women are made in God's image (Gen. 1:27), and therefore they are more like God than anything else in all creation. Human beings are intended to live as God's created analogy for his own glory. God did not create humans because of any need within himself (Job 41:11; Ps. 50:9–12; Acts 17:24–25) but primarily so that he would be glorified in them as they delight in him and reflect his character. We were created primarily to be in relationship with our Creator and find our greatest joy in him. When people are supremely satisfied in him, God is rightly honored and delights in his creation. God describes his people as "everyone who is called by my name, *whom I created for my glory*, whom I formed and made" (Isa. 43:7; see Eph. 1:11–12).

Although God has no unmet needs, humans bring delight to his heart as they trust and obey him.

> You shall be a crown of beauty in the hand of the LORD,
>   and a royal diadem in the hand of your God. . . .
> As the bridegroom rejoices over the bride,
>   so shall your God rejoice over you. (Isa. 62:3–5)

> The LORD your God is in your midst . . .
> he will rejoice over you with gladness . . .
> he will exult over you with loud singing. (Zeph. 3:17)

God's delight in the Spirit-empowered faithfulness of his people is the believer's greatest motive for holy living in the Christian life. Unbiblical motives for obeying God's commands include pragmatism, legalism, utilitarianism, and man-centeredness. But our deepest desire should be to find our greatest joy in bringing joy to the heart of our Creator.

IMPLICATIONS OF BEING CREATED IN GOD'S IMAGE FOR HIS GLORY

Humility, Purpose, and Accountability

When human beings acknowledge God as the Creator of everything, we rightly recognize him as the One upon whom we are utterly dependent for all we are and have. Nothing exists apart from the creative and sustaining power of God, and all things owe honor and submission to him. This dependence should lead to deep humility and accountability before the God who made us (Rom. 9:20–21). God's personal creation of all humans (Ps. 139:13–16) is the basis for human purpose and meaning. His act of creation leads us to recognize him as majestic and great and to acknowledge that we are very small before him. When people truly understand God as Creator, they recognize that he is eternal, powerful, wise, good, the owner of all things, and the judge of all. Because God is Creator, all people must answer to him; he, however, need not answer to anyone: "But who are you, O man, to answer back to God? Will what is molded say to its molder, 'Why have you made me like this?' Has the potter no right over the clay, to make out of the same lump one vessel for honorable use and another for dishonorable use?" (Rom. 9:20–21).

Seeing the Gifts and Glory of God in Creation
At the culmination of God's creation he declared it to be "very good" (Gen. 1:31), but it was later marred and distorted by the fall and God's curse (Genesis 3; Rom. 8:20–23). Nevertheless, the heavens continue to declare the glory of God (Ps. 19:1–14), God continues to give bountiful gifts to be gratefully enjoyed (1 Tim. 6:17), and God's image-bearers are encouraged to see and glorify him in all things (1 Cor. 10:31).

Hope Due to God's Creative Work and Power
The New Testament compares God's work of redemption with his work in creation: "For God, who said, 'Let light shine out of darkness,' has shone in our hearts to give the light of the knowledge of the glory of God in the face of Jesus Christ" (2 Cor. 4:6). When God redeems someone, he is re-creating with the same power with which he spoke the world into existence (2 Cor. 5:17; Eph. 2:10). God is the powerful, wise, good God who made everything; knowing this provides great hope for personal and cosmic transformation. There is never room for a believer to despair over his or her own level of sanctification, nor is it legitimate to doubt God's ability

to change someone we are ministering to, because God's power as Creator is fully able to change rebellious hearts into worshipful ones. We can also be sure that this fallen and cursed world will one day be made new by the One who created it in the first place.

Philosophy of Ministry

Because God created everything with his glory as the ultimate goal, bringing honor to his name is the appropriate, explicit, overarching objective of all life and ministry: "So, whether you eat or drink, or whatever you do, do all to the glory of God" (1 Cor. 10:31). When planning a worship service or church program, thinking through a business plan, raising a family, creating art, or running a farm, the fundamental question must always be, will God be glorified?

MAN MADE IN THE IMAGE OF GOD

Man is made in the image of God, which means that he is like God and represents God on the earth:

> Then God said, "Let us make man *in our image, after our likeness.* And let them have dominion over the fish of the sea and over the birds of the heavens and over the livestock and over all the earth and over every creeping thing that creeps on the earth."
>
> So God created man *in his own image,*
> *in the image of God* he created him;
> male and female he created them. (Gen. 1:26–27)

While everything in creation to some degree reflects something of who God is (Ps. 19:1–6), humans stand alone as made in the image and likeness of God. People are intended to live as God's created analogies, showing his character more clearly than anything else. Being made in the image of God distinguishes mankind from all other living things.

While humans are the pinnacle of creation, to say we are *like* God also means that we are not and will never *be* God. We have great dignity because we are made in God's image, but our worth is not self-made. God is the source of all human value. Thus, John Calvin says: "We are not to consider that men merit of themselves but look upon the image of God in all men, to which we owe all honor and love."[1]

The fall and curse of humanity distorts the image of God in man but does not remove it from him. After the fall, the image of God remains the basis for human dignity and biblical ethics (Gen. 9:6; James 3:8–9).

The image of God is evident in our unique spiritual, moral, mental, relational, and physical capacities. Humans reflect the image of God in varying degrees and ways, but no one is made in *more* of God's image or *less* of God's image. The foundation of Christian ethics is the assumption that *all* humans are made in God's image regardless of the presence or absence of certain abilities. From conception to death all human beings are God's image-bearers, and all are creatures of profound dignity and value, equally worthy of protection and respect. The value of human life is not affected or determined by age, disability, race, intellectual ability, emotional or mental state, relational powers, or gender.

The Great Commandment—to love God with all our heart, soul, mind, and strength—obviously entails the second greatest commandment: to love our neighbor as ourselves (Matt. 22:37–40). Love for God *must* be expressed in love for people, even one's enemies (Luke 6:27): "If anyone says, 'I love God,' and hates his brother, he is a liar; for he who does not love his brother whom he has seen cannot love God whom he has not seen. And this

---

[1]John Calvin, *Institutes of the Christian Religion*, bk. 3, ch. 7, section 6.

134

commandment we have from him: *whoever loves God must also love his brother*" (1 John 4:20–21). Christians are called to see beyond mankind's fallen condition to the image of God in the people they interact with every day, and to love them based on what God says is true of them. This means they no longer regard anyone from a worldly point of view but rather see them with God's eyes: "From now on, therefore, we regard no one *according to the flesh*. Even though we once regarded Christ *according to the flesh*, we regard him thus no longer" (2 Cor. 5:16).

Jesus, who in his divinity is the image of the invisible God (2 Cor. 4:4; Col. 1:15), perfectly reflects the divine image within his true humanity and holy life on earth. Jesus shows perfect humanness in his perfect fellowship with and obedience to the Father, which leads to his selfless love for others. These characteristics of Christ's life are foundational to all other God-glorifying manifestations of the image of God in humanity. Therefore, to experience true humanity, God's people should pattern their lives after Jesus's exemplary relationship to God the Father. In this way, they will be conformed more and more to the image of Christ (Rom. 8:29; see 1 John 3:2).

THE CONSTITUTIONAL MAKE-UP OF HUMAN BEINGS

Biblically, there are at least two distinct aspects of a human being—spiritual (spirit/soul) and physical (body). Some interpreters hold that the "soul" and "spirit" are distinct parts of a human being, and therefore that we are composed of three parts: body, soul, and spirit. This view is called "trichotomy." However, the vast majority of evangelical scholars today hold that "spirit" and "soul" are basically synonymous and are two different ways of talking about the immaterial aspect of our being: "soul" points to our personal selves as responsible individuals and "spirit" points to those same selves as created by and dependent on God. This view is called "dichotomy." It is important to see that there is a fundamental unity between the physical and spiritual within humans. While a distinction is made in the Bible between the material and immaterial parts of the human being, the emphasis is on the necessary connection between body and soul. Regeneration and sanctification for the Christian is a spiritual experience intended to be expressed in the physical body in and through which we have been made to live. The separation of body and soul caused at death is an unnatural tragedy, which will be remedied when the body is resurrected, allowing humans to exist as they were intended to do.

HUMANITY AS MALE AND FEMALE

God made man (Hebrew, *'adam*) as male and female from the beginning, completely equal in their value and in their full humanity (Gen. 1:26–27; 9:6), and yet distinct in the way they relate and function. The distinct roles of men and women are grounded in the nature of God (1 Cor. 11:3) and were part of God's very good creation before the fall (1 Cor. 11:8–10; 1 Tim. 2:13). These role distinctions in no way minimize the worth of men or women. Both are equally made in God's image, equally fallen (Genesis 3; Rom. 3:23), equally redeemable (Gal. 3:28; 1 Pet. 3:7), and they are equally to be resurrected and glorified (1 John 3:2). This equality is expressed, however, with the husband serving in his God-ordained role as authority and servant leader (Gen. 2:23) and with the wife fulfilling her vital role as supporter and helper (Gen. 2:18; 1 Pet. 3:1–6) in the family and the church. Male authority is to be exercised with love, humility, and respect, under the authority of Christ (Eph. 5:25–33; Col. 3:19; 1 Pet. 3:7). Female submission is not servile weakness but rather a display of strength and trust in God, as the woman uses all her God-given abilities while refusing to usurp the male authority in her life (Eph. 5:22–25; Col. 3:18; 1 Tim. 2:12; 3:2; Titus 2:4–5; 1 Pet. 3:1–6). The fall greatly distorted the harmonious yet distinct way men and women were intended to function together (Gen. 3:16). God's people are still called to show the world how men and women are meant to relate in mutually beneficial ways for the glory of God. When men and women function in this complementary way, they display something profoundly and mysteriously like the relationship between Jesus and his bride, the church. After quoting Genesis 2:24, which refers to the marriage between Adam and Eve as God originally created it, Paul explains that God's purpose for marriage is to be a picture of Christ and his church (Eph. 5:32).

SCRIPTURE MEMORY AND MEDITATION

So God created man in his own image,
in the image of God he created him;
male and female he created them. (Gen. 1:27)

Questions for Application and Discussion

1. How does being a creature, dependent on God for your very existence, make you think differently about yourself and your relationship with him?

2. How does thinking about humans as being made in God's image modify the way you treat yourself and others? What influence should this doctrine have on issues like racism, pornography, war, eating disorders, government, and education?

3. Because of the Christian belief that all humans are sinful, do you think you may have neglected the wonder, dignity, and reverence we should have for humans, who are made in God's image?

4. Have you been taught that humans comprise three parts, body, soul, and spirit? Do you think anything

is lost if we are only two parts, and that soul and spirit are not distinct entities? Do you appreciate the fundamental and intended interrelationship between the body and soul? What might be detrimental results of overly separating body and soul?

5. Have you seen good examples of biblically defined manhood and womanhood? If so, describe them. What experiences and feelings do you bring to the discussion of gender? What would be the benefits of functioning well as men and women together for the glory of God?

For Further Study

Berkouwer, G. C. *Man: The Image of God.* Grand Rapids, MI: Eerdmans, 1962.

Clouse, Bonnidell, and Robert G. Clouse, eds. *Women in Ministry: Four Views.* Downers Grove, IL: InterVarsity Press, 1989.

Hoekema, Anthony A. *Created in God's Image.* Grand Rapids, MI: Eerdmans and Exeter, UK: Paternoster, 1986, pp. 1–111.

Johnson, Philip, *Darwin on Trial.* Downers Grove, IL: InterVarsity, 1993.

Kassian, Mary A. *Women, Creation, and the Fall.* Westchester, IL: Crossway, 1990.

Piper, John. *What's the Difference? Manhood and Womanhood Defined according to the Bible.* Westchester, IL: Crossway, 1990.

Piper, John, and Wayne Grudem, eds. *Recovering Biblical Manhood and Womanhood: A Response to Evangelical Feminism.* Westchester, IL: Crossway, 1991.

Piper, John, and Justin Taylor. *Sex and the Supremacy of Christ.* Wheaton, IL: Crossway, 2005.

Sherlock, Charles. *The Doctrine of Humanity.* Contours of Christian Theology. Downers Grove, IL: InterVarsity Press, 1997.

HOW DOES GOD RELATE TO HIS CREATION?

"Behind a frowning providence, He hides a smiling face." —William Cowper

TRANSCENDENCE AND IMMANENCE

God is both transcendent (majestic and holy, far greater than his creatures) and immanent (near and present, fully involved with his creatures). To understand the God of the Bible, this vital biblical balance must be appreciated. God is distinct from and far above all he has made: "The LORD is high above all nations, and his glory above the heavens! Who is like the LORD our God, who is seated on high, who looks far down on the heavens and the earth?" (Ps. 113:4–6). Yet he is also always actively, personally engaged with his creation: "Yet he is actually not far from each one of us, for 'In him we live and move and have our being'; as even some of your own poets have said, 'For we are indeed his offspring'" (Acts 17:27–28). Those most humbled by God's majesty and holiness most experience personal closeness with him: "For thus says the One who is high and lifted up, who inhabits eternity, whose name is Holy: 'I dwell in the high and holy place [transcendence], and also with him who is of a contrite and lowly spirit, to revive the spirit of the lowly, and to revive the heart of the contrite [immanence]'" (Isa. 57:15).

Non-Christian religions tend toward one extreme or the other—either to a god who is so "other than" creation that nothing meaningful can be said about him (e.g., Eastern and New Age religions) or to one who is so "identified with" creation that his majestic holiness is lost (e.g., Greco-Roman and much current Western religion). An accurate understanding of God deeply appreciates both his awesome otherness and his intimate nearness. Christians relate to a God who is both the great "I AM" and the "God of our fathers" (Ex. 3:14–15). He is the eternal, infinite God who has stepped not only into time and space but also into covenant relationship with his people through the incarnation of Christ. The biblical balance between God's transcendence and his immanence is hard to maintain, but the best worship, prayer, and daily relating to God are those which have in them a deep recognition of both God's majestic holiness and his personal engagement with the creatures he has made.

THE PROVIDENCE OF GOD

God is always personally involved with his creation in sustaining and preserving it, and acting within it to bring about his own perfect goals. Everything that takes place is under God's control. He "works all things according to the counsel of his will" (Eph. 1:11). His providential dominion is over all things (Prov. 16:9; 19:21; James 4:13–15), such as weather (Job 38:22–30), food (Ps. 145:15), and sparrows (Matt. 10:29), as well as kings (Prov. 21:1), kingdoms (Dan. 4:25), and the exact times and places in which people live (Acts 17:26). Salvation is a work of God's governing power: "For by grace you have been saved through faith. And this is not your own doing; it is the gift of God, not a result of works, so that no one may boast" (Eph. 2:8–9; see Ezek. 36:24; John 6:37–40; Acts 13:48; 16:14; Rom. 9:16; Phil. 1:29; 2 Pet. 1:1). God's providential power also brings about sanctification (Phil. 2:12–13) and fruitfulness in ministry (Col. 1:28–29).

God is able to work out his sovereign will within the distinctive characteristics of what he has created. He moves a rock as a rock, and he moves a human heart as a human heart. He does not turn a person into a thing when he brings about his sovereign intentions in a person's life. Paul describes sanctification as the result of both human effort and ultimate divine enabling when he commands believers to "work out your own salvation with fear and trembling, for it is God who works in you, both to will and to work for his good pleasure" (Phil. 2:12–13). He sees no conflict between divine and human activity. Rather, God is uniquely able to bring about his purposes within human beings so that they are fully engaged as persons and responsible for their own decisions, attitudes, and actions.

GOD'S RELATIONSHIP TO EVIL

God controls and uses evil but is never morally blameworthy for it (Ex. 4:11; Deut. 32:39; Isa. 45:7; Amos 3:6). However God's relationship to evil is understood, both his complete sovereignty and his complete holiness must be maintained. In his great suffering, Job says, "The LORD gave, and the LORD has taken away; blessed be the name of the LORD" (Job 1:21). We are told that Job's assessment of God's providence over evil is correct in that "in all this Job did not sin or charge God with wrong" (Job 1:22). Joseph expresses a similar attitude of the God-ordained evil actions of his brothers toward him when he says, "as for you, *you meant evil* against me, but *God meant it for good*, to bring it about that many people should be kept alive, as they are today" (Gen. 50:20). The greatest evil ever done, the crucifixion of Christ, happened because of unspeakable human sin, but it was all within God's perfect plan: "This Jesus, delivered up *according to the definite plan and foreknowledge of God*, you crucified and *killed by the hands of lawless men*" (Acts 2:23; see Acts 4:27–28). Even human rebellion unintentionally ends up serving the perfectly wise purposes of God. Nothing—not even sin and great evil—can ever ultimately frustrate God's sovereignty. Christians can be sure that God will one day defeat all sin, evil, and suffering. Until then, God can be trusted, even when in the short term it may not seem to be so from our earthly, human perspective because he is wise, holy, sovereign, and powerful and is always working out his plan to perfection (Rom. 8:28).

SCRIPTURE MEMORY AND MEDITATION

For thus says the One who is high and lifted up,
  who inhabits eternity, whose name is Holy:
"I dwell in the high and holy place,
  and also with him who is of a contrite and lowly spirit,
to revive the spirit of the lowly,
  and to revive the heart of the contrite."
  (Isa. 57:15)

Questions for Application and Discussion

1. Have you emphasized either God's transcendence or immanence in your understanding of him? How has this chapter helped to balance your thinking? Has your church experience given you a balanced view of

God's transcendence and immanence? What are ways to make sure you appreciate both his majesty and his relational characteristics?

2. Is the providence of God a troubling or a comforting idea for you? How would a full understanding of God's wisdom provide trust in God's providence?

3. In light of God's providence, are there ways you think too much in terms of luck and superstition rather than in God's sovereign control of all things?

4. What blessings in your life do you take for granted? How should the doctrine of providence increase your gratitude to God?

5. In the past, how have you tried to reconcile God's providence and the reality of evil in the world? In light of the biblical evidence for God's control over all things presented in this chapter, do you think you have recognized God's sovereignty enough? Does it help you to reconcile providence and evil by understanding that the evil of the cross of Christ is also the way God redeems sinners?

For Further Study

Basinger, David, and Randall Basinger, eds. *Predestination and Free Will: Four Views of Divine Sovereignty and Human Freedom.* Downers Grove, IL: InterVarsity Press, 1986.

Berkouwer, G. C. *The Providence of God.* Translated by Lewis B. Smedes. Grand Rapids, MI: Eerdmans, 1952.

Carson, D. A. *Divine Sovereignty and Human Responsibility: Biblical Perspectives in Tension.* New Foundations Theological Library. Atlanta: John Knox, 1981, and Grand Rapids, MI: Baker, 1994.

———. *How Long, O Lord? Reflections on Suffering and Evil.* Grand Rapids, MI: Baker, 1990.

Craig, William Lane. *The Only Wise God: The Compatibility of Divine Foreknowledge and Human Freedom*. Grand Rapids, MI: Baker, 1987.

Feinberg, John. *The Many Faces of Evil: Theological Systems and the Problem of Evil*. Zondervan, 1994.

Flavel, John. *The Mystery of Providence*. Carlisle, PA: Banner of Truth, 1976. Reprint of 1698 ed.

Helm, Paul. *The Providence of God*. Downers Grove, IL: InterVarsity Press, 1994.

Packer, J. I. *Evangelism and the Sovereignty of God*. Downers Grove, IL: IVP Academic, 1991.

Pinnock, Clark, ed. *The Grace of God, the Will of Man*. Grand Rapids, MI: Zondervan, 1989.

Spiegel, James. *The Benefits of Providence: A New Look at Divine Sovereignty*. Wheaton, IL: Crossway, 2005.

WHAT IS
SIN?

"Pride lifts up the heart against God. It contends for the supremacy with him. How unseemly moreover is this sin. A creature so utterly dependent, so fearfully guilty, yet proud in heart." —Charles Bridges

BIBLICAL TERMS FOR SIN

The Bible explains human rebellion against God from several perspectives and with various images:

- doing evil (Judg. 2:11)
- disobedience (Rom. 5:19)
- transgression (Ex. 23:21; see 1 Tim. 2:14)
- iniquity (Lev. 26:40)
- lawlessness (Titus 2:14; 1 John 3:4)
- trespass (Eph. 2:1)
- ungodliness (1 Pet. 4:18)

- unrighteousness (1 John 1:9)
- unholy (1 Tim. 1:9)
- wickedness (Prov. 11:31)

THE DEFINITION OF SIN

Sin is anything (whether in thoughts, actions, or attitudes) that does not express or conform to the holy character of God as revealed in his moral law. It includes the following five elements.

1. *Sin is moral evil* (e.g., murder) as opposed to natural evil (e.g., cancer). Moral evil is personal rebellion against God, and it is what brought natural evil into the world.

2. *Sin is always and ultimately related to God.* While sin has devastating societal, relational, and physical ramifications, the central problem of sin is that it offends and incurs his wrath. David demonstrates this understanding in his confession of adultery and murder: "Against you, you only, have I sinned and done what is evil in your sight, so that you may be justified in your words and blameless in your judgment" (Ps. 51:4). This is not to minimize his sin against Bathsheba, her husband Uriah, or the people of Israel, but rather to recognize that, relatively speaking, it is God he has ultimately offended, and it is to God alone that he must finally answer. Sin is a personal attack on the character and ordinances of God.

3. *Sin is breaking God's law*, which can take several forms. There are sins of omission (not doing what we should) as well as sins of commission (doing what we should not do). Breaking one of God's commandments is rebellion against the entire character of God, and in that sense it is equivalent to breaking all of the commandments: "For whoever keeps the whole law but fails in one point has become accountable for all of it" (James 2:10; see Gal. 3:10). God's unified law is a reflection of his personal nature and claims, which means that rejecting one of his laws amounts to rejecting him.

146

Although breaking one commandment makes one guilty of breaking God's entire law, God recognizes that there are gradations of sin. These gradations are based on differences in *knowledge* (Ezek. 8:6, 13; Matt. 10:15; Luke 12:47–48; John 19:11), *intent* (Num. 15:30–31), *kind*, and *effect*. Nevertheless, even sin done in ignorance is still sin needing forgiveness. While God recognizes degrees of sin on a human, ethical level, it remains the case that all people are equally guilty before God and equally in need of Christ's atoning work.

4. *Sin is rooted deep in our very nature*, and sinful actions reveal the condition of a depraved heart within: "Out of the heart come evil thoughts, murder, adultery, sexual immorality, theft, false witness, slander" (Matt. 15:19; see Matt. 7:15–19). Internal attitudes are frequently identified as sinful or righteous in the Bible, and God demands not only correct outward actions but also that the heart be right (Ex. 20:17; Heb. 13:5).

5. Sin has brought about a *guilty standing before God* and a *corrupted condition* in all humans. The pronouncement of guilt is God's legal determination that people are in an unrighteous state before him, and the condition of corruption is our polluted state, which inclines us toward ungodly behavior. By the grace of God, both this inherited guilt and this inherited moral pollution are atoned for by Christ: "If we confess our sins, he is faithful and just to forgive us our sins and to cleanse us from all unrighteousness" (1 John 1:9).

THE ORIGIN OF SIN

Sin entered the human race in the garden of Eden through an attack of Satan, who led Adam and Eve to doubt God's word and trust their own ability to discern good and evil (Genesis 3). Sometime prior to this, Satan (a fallen angel) must himself have rebelled against God and become evil, though Scripture says little about that event (2 Pet. 2:4; Jude 6). Satan's strategy was to bring disorder to the created order by approaching Eve and getting her to lead her husband away from God. Adam, so it appears, allowed his wife to be deceived by failing to take up his God-ordained responsibility to lead and protect her. Satan then questioned God's goodness, wisdom, and care for Adam and Eve by suggesting that God was a miserly legalist in his prohibition of the fruit of the tree of the knowledge of good and evil. Satan then simply lied, saying, "You will not surely die" (Gen. 3:4). Such deception and rebellion against God stem from a failure to trust him and be satisfied with him and his commands and ways. Satan and our first parents demanded autonomy and rejected God's authority, and this has been the source and shape of human sin ever since. Unbelief (Rom. 14:23; Heb. 11:6), pride, and selfishness lead us to think we know better than God and to try to put ourselves in his place. All people, in their fallen condition, are indeed "lovers of self . . . rather than lovers of God" (2 Tim. 2:2, 4).

THE CONSEQUENCES AND CONDITION OF THE FALL

God rightly judged the rebellion of Adam and Eve and brought a curse on them and all their offspring. The curse brought physical and spiritual death, separation from God, and alienation from him and others. All people are now conceived, born, and live in this fallen, depraved condition: "None is righteous, no, not one; no one understands; no one seeks for God. All have turned aside; together they have become worthless; no one does good, not even one" (Rom. 3:10–12); "All we like sheep have gone astray; we have turned—every one—to his own way; and the LORD has laid on him the iniquity of us all" (Isa. 53:6).

Inherited guilt and corruption leave every person completely unable to save himself or to please God. There are at least six ways this pervasive inability affects everyone. Until God intervenes with his sovereign, gracious, saving power, mankind is totally unable to:

- repent or trust Christ (John 6:44; see John 3:3; 6:65);
- see or enter the kingdom of God (John 3:3);
- obey God and thereby glorify him (Rom. 8:6–8);
- attain spiritual understanding (1 Cor. 2:14);
- live lives pleasing to God (Rom. 14:23; Heb. 11:6);
- receive eternal or spiritual life (Eph. 2:1–3).

Because of God's common grace (that is, his kindly providence whereby sin's energies within us are partly restrained), total depravity does not mean that every person apart from Christ is as bad as possible. It does mean, however, that no one by nature can fulfill man's primary purpose of glorifying God in relationship with him.

SCRIPTURE MEMORY AND MEDITATION

"For all have sinned and fall short of the glory of God, and are justified by his grace as a gift, through the redemption that is in Christ Jesus." (Rom. 3:23–24)

Questions for Application and Discussion

1. How has this chapter shaped your understanding of sin? Has it made you aware of your own sin in any new way?

2. Because sin is a violation of God's moral law, which is a reflection of his character, how should that influence your hatred of sin? Do you grieve over your sin?

3. What should be your main motive for overcoming temptation? What are poor motives for refraining from sin?

4. Is it hard for you to believe that all humans are sinful? If so, why? What might be missing in your understanding of God or people if you don't see all people as needing forgiveness?

5. Do you struggle with the fairness of inheriting sin from Adam? Do you wish you could have had your turn in the garden of Eden to overcome temptation rather than being implicated in Adam's sin? How might your struggle change if you were to grow in your trust of God's all-knowing wisdom?

For Further Study

Jenson, Matt. *The Gravity of Sin: Augustine, Luther, and Barth on homo incurvatus in se*. New York: T&T Clark, 2006.

Lewis, C. S. *The Problem of Pain*. New York: Macmillan, 1962.

Murray, John. *The Imputation of Adam's Sin*. Grand Rapids, MI: Eerdmans, 1959.

Plantinga, Cornelius, Jr., *Not the Way It's Supposed to Be: A Breviary of Sin*. Grand Rapids, MI: Eerdmans, 1995.

Wenham, J. W. *The Enigma of Evil*. Grand Rapids, MI: Zondervan, 1985. Formerly published as *The Goodness of God*.

HOW DOES GOD
SAVE SINNERS?

*"It is not your hold on Christ that saves you; it is Christ.
It is not your joy in Christ that saves you; it is Christ.
It is not even your faith in Christ, though that be the
instrument; it is Christ's blood and merit."*
—Charles Spurgeon

The concept of "salvation" (Greek, *sōtēria*) as it is used throughout the Bible can embrace the broad range of God's activity in rescuing people from sin and restoring them to a right relationship with himself. Because of this broad sense, we find that the noun *salvation* and the verb *save* are used in the Bible with past, present, and future reference.

Thus, salvation may signify any or all of the blessings outlined in figure 14.1. While the *subjective experience* of being saved may have degrees and look very different from person to person, the *objective state* of being saved is categorical and absolute.

From God's perspective there is a definite point in time when those who have trusted in Christ pass from death into life (1 John 3:14). This, however, is not where salvation starts. From God's vantage point salvation begins with his *election* of individuals, which is his determination beforehand that his saving purpose will be accomplished in them (John 6:37–39, 44, 64–66; 8:47; 10:26; 15:16; Acts 13:48; 16:14; Romans 9; 1 John 4:19; 5:1). God then in due course *brings* people to himself by *calling* them to faith in Christ (Rom. 8:30; 1 Cor. 1:9; 2 Tim. 1:9; 1 Pet. 2:9).

Fig. 14.1

THE BLESSINGS OF SALVATION

Justification	has been saved	from the guilt of sin	Eph. 2:8
Sanctification	is being saved	from the power of sin	1 Cor. 1:18
Glorification	will be saved	from the presence of sin	Acts 15:11

God's calling produces *regeneration*; this miraculous work of the Holy Spirit makes a spiritually dead person alive in Christ (Ezek. 11:19–20; Matt. 19:28; John 3:3, 5, 7; Titus 3:5). The revived heart *repents* and trusts Christ in *saving faith* as the only source of *justification*. To be a Christian means one has traded in his "polluted garment" of self-righteousness for the perfect righteousness of Christ (Phil. 3:8–9; see Isa. 64:6). He has ceased striving and now rests in the finished work of Christ—no longer depending on personal accomplishments, religious pedigree, or good works for God's approval, but only on what Christ has accomplished on his behalf (Eph. 2:8–9). A Christian understands with Paul that "it is no longer I who live, but Christ who lives in me. And the life I now live in the flesh I live by faith in the Son of God, who loved me and gave himself for me" (Gal. 2:20). Concerning Jesus paying the penalty for our sins, the Christian believes that when Jesus said, "It is finished" (John 19:30), it really was. Because of this, "there is therefore now no condemnation for those who are in Christ Jesus" (Rom. 8:1), and they have been "saved to the uttermost . . ." (Heb. 7:25). A miraculous transformation has taken place in which the believer has "passed from death to life" (John 5:24). The Holy Spirit empowers the transformation from rebellious sinner to humble worshiper, leading to "confidence for the day of judgment . . ." (1 John 4:17).

Much of Protestantism in the last two centuries has been influenced by revivalism, which puts a great emphasis on "making a decision for Christ" in a public and definitive way. These "moments of decision" often come to be treated as the crucial evidence that one is truly saved. Other Protestant traditions, less influenced by revivalism, are often content to leave the conversion experience less clearly identified, and put the focus instead on Christian experience, identification with the church, or reliance upon the sacraments. Both of these traditions have benefits and strengths, as well as potential problems. The "decision" approach rightly emphasizes the need for personal commitment to Christ and the idea that regeneration takes place at a specific time. The potential downside is that this view can lead to a simplistic, human-centered understanding of being saved, where one depends too heavily on the initial, specific act of trusting Christ as the primary evidence of conversion. As a result, one can doubt that the "decision" was real, leading to numerous journeys down the aisle ("just in case"), or to total dependence on the one-time walk down the aisle, even in the absence of the necessary fruit of salvation. Other traditions appreciate the sovereignty of God and the role of the church in the salvation process but can leave conversion so vague that the need for personal trust in Christ and the resulting evidence of a changed life can be neglected.

God uses vastly different circumstances and experiences to bring people to himself. As C. H. Spurgeon said, "God's Spirit calls men to Jesus in different ways. Some are drawn so gently that they scarcely know when the drawing began. Others are so suddenly affected that their conversion stands out with noonday clearness."[1] The best evidence of true salvation is not having raised a hand or prayed a prayer, *or* having been baptized or christened. Instead, the true test of an authentic work of God in one's life is *sanctification* as God continues the moral transformation he began in regeneration. This transformation will continue until the redeemed person is *resurrected* and made completely holy in heaven (*glorification*; see Rom. 8:28–30; Phil. 1:6; 1 John 3:2).

God's sanctifying work is seen in growing Christlike character, increasing love for God and people, and the fruit of the Spirit (John 15:1–16:33; Gal. 5:22–25; James 2:18). Of course, a memorable conversion experience may serve as an important reference point for a saving work of God in one's life, but it is only the obvious, ongoing work of the Holy Spirit in making one more and more like Jesus that gives sufficiently clear indication that a person has been made a new creation in Christ. While a Christian should never be satisfied with his current state of holiness, he should be confident that through God's sovereign, sanctifying grace he will one day have total victory over sin. This will be the moment of entering by death into a larger life in which his sinful heart is finally purified. Meanwhile, living with this hope as one battles sin daily is true Christian *perseverance* (1 Cor. 1:8–9; Eph. 1:13–14; 1 Thess. 5:23–24; 1 Pet. 1:4–5; 1 John 2:19; Jude 1, 24–25), which is itself a sign that one has been born again.

SCRIPTURE MEMORY AND MEDITATION

"For those whom he foreknew he also predestined to
be conformed to the image of his Son, in order that

---

[1]Charles Haddon Spurgeon, "Is Conversion Necessary?" (sermon 1183, Metropolitan Tabernacle, Newington, July 19,1874).

he might be the firstborn among many brothers. And those whom he predestined he also called, and those whom he called he also justified, and those whom he justified he also glorified." (Rom. 8:29–30)

Questions for Application and Discussion

1. What do you think of the doctrine of election? Do you think God elected sinners for salvation because he knew they would choose him or because of his determination apart from anything in us? What outcomes could your answer to this question have on your relationship with God and growth in Christ?

2. Have you been born again? If so, what in your life shows that your conversion was real and that you are truly born again? How can you tell the difference between mere religious activity and true Spirit-enabled life in Christ?

3. If you have not trusted Christ for forgiveness of your sins, what is keeping you from doing so? Do you have mostly intellectual, moral, emotional, or relational difficulties with being a Christian, or is there something else? What would it take for you to become a Christian? What about Jesus makes him unworthy of your trust?

4. Have you ever experienced true sorrow for your sin? What is the difference between being truly sorry for sin and just being sorry for the practical ramifications of it? What is the difference between being sorry you got caught for sin and having a God-centered understanding of sin? What are elements of true repentance?

5. How do you feel when you think that not only can you have your sins forgiven, but that by faith you can have

the righteousness of Christ given to you? Does being adopted into God's family through faith in Christ increase your sense of security in your relationship with God?

For Further Study

Alexander, Donald L., ed. *Christian Spirituality: Five Views of Sanctification*. Downers Grove, IL: InterVarsity Press, 1988.

Boice, James M., and Philip G. Ryken. *The Doctrines of Grace: Rediscovering the Evangelical Gospel*. Wheaton, IL: Crossway, 2009.

Burke, Trevor. *Adopted into God's Family: Exploring a Pauline Metaphor*. Downers Grove, IL: IVP, 2006.

Clotfelter, David. *Sinners in the Hands of a Good God: Reconciling Divine Judgment and Mercy*. Chicago: Moody, 2004.

Coleman, Robert E. *The Master Plan of Evangelism*. Abridged 2nd ed. Grand Rapids, MI: Spire, 1994.

Demarest, Bruce. *The Cross and Salvation: The Doctrine of Salvation*. Wheaton, IL: Crossway, 2006.

Lloyd-Jones, D. Martyn. *Spiritual Depression: Its Causes and Cures*. Grand Rapids, MI: Eerdmans, 1965.

Packer, J. I. *Evangelism and the Sovereignty of God*. Downers Grove, IL: InterVarsity Press, 1961.

_____. *Keep in Step with the Spirit*. Old Tappan, NJ: Revell, 1984.

Peterson, Robert A. *Election and Free Will: God's Gracious Choice and Our Responsibility*. Phillipsburg, NJ: P&R, 2007.

Pinnock, Clark H., ed. *Grace Unlimited*. Minneapolis: Bethany, 1975.

_____. *The Grace of God, the Will of Man: A Case for Arminianism*. Grand Rapids, MI: Zondervan, 1989.

Piper, John. *Finally Alive: What Happens When We Are Born Again*. Fearn, Ross-shire, Scotland: Christian Focus, 2009.

Schreiner, Thomas, and Bruce Ware, eds. *The Grace of God, the Bondage of the Will: A Case for Calvinism*. Grand Rapids, MI: Baker, 1995.

Storms, C. Samuel. *Chosen for Life: The Case for Divine Election*. Wheaton, IL: Crossway, 2007.

Stott, John. *Baptism and Fullness*. Leicester and Downers Grove, IL: InterVarsity Press, 1976.

Watson, Thomas. *The Doctrine of Repentance*. Carlisle, PA: Banner of Truth, 1987.

Willard, Dallas. *The Spirit of the Disciplines: Understanding How God Changes Lives*. San Francisco: Harper & Row, 1988.

WHAT IS
THE CHURCH?

"Our Lord Jesus Christ is the sun about which the whole mission of the church revolves. Public worship is the encounter of the risen Redeemer with his people; evangelism is calling men to the Savior; publishing the law of God is proclaiming his lordship; Christian nurture is feeding his lambs and disciplining his flock; ministering to the needs of men is continuing the work of the Great Physician." —R. G. Clouse

The church is the community of God's redeemed people—all who have truly trusted Christ alone for their salvation. It is created by the Holy Spirit to exalt Jesus Christ as Lord of all. Christ is the Head, Savior, Lord, and King of the church. The relationship between its members results from their common identity as brothers and sisters adopted into God's family.

The identity of this family is grounded in Christ's person and work and therefore transcends any earthly distinctions of race, class, culture, gender, or nationality. True Christian fellowship is divinely brought about by God, for the purpose of displaying and advancing God's kingdom on earth. As Christians love one another and submit to the lordship of Christ, they show glimpses of heavenly realities that are to come.

There is ultimately only one church, the global community of believers on earth plus those already in glory. In this world, however, the one church takes the form of countless local churches, each of which must be viewed as a microcosm, outcropping, and sample of the larger whole. Jesus Christ's headship of the church that is his body is a relationship that applies both to the universal church and to each local church. Denominational identities are secondary to these primary and fundamental realities.

THE VISIBLE CHURCH AND THE INVISIBLE CHURCH

Theologians sometimes distinguish between the "visible church" (the church as Christians on earth see it) and the "invisible church" (the church as God in heaven sees it). This distinction emphasizes two truths. First, only God, who reads hearts, knows the ultimate makeup of the "invisible church"—those whom he has called ("The Lord knows those who are his . . ." [2 Tim. 2:19]). Second, there are some within the "visible church" who are not genuine believers, though they may look as if they are (see Matt. 7:15–16; Acts 20:29–30; 1 John 2:19).

IMAGES OF THE CHURCH

The Bible explains the profound mystery of the church (Eph. 5:32) using varied images and illustrations. Among the most important are the church as the building, body, bride, and family of Christ.

The Building of Christ

Jesus Christ is building his church, and even the gates of hell will not defeat it (Matt. 16:18). He is the foundational cornerstone providing unyielding stability (Matt. 21:42; Acts 4:11; Eph. 2:20; 1 Pet. 2:6–7), and he promises that he will complete the building he is making (Eph. 2:21–22). Therefore, even when the church appears weak, corrupt, and lost, there is always reason for deep confidence in its continued growth and enduring strength. God's people are "living stones" (1 Pet. 2:5) who have received their life from the Cornerstone, who is the giver of life. The building image is grounded in the temple imagery of the Old Testament; the temple was the place where God's presence and glory were most often seen. The church is now the place on earth where God primarily dwells and makes himself known. This temple is not made with human hands but exists in the corporate life of those who have been transformed through faith in Christ. The presence and work of God in worship, the ministry of the Word, service to others, discipline, baptism, the Lord's Supper, and gospel proclamation are now the primary source of the presence and glory of God in the world: "Do you not know that you are God's temple and that God's Spirit dwells in you? If anyone destroys God's temple, God will destroy him. For God's temple is holy, and you are that temple" (1 Cor. 3:16–17; see 2 Cor. 6:16; 1 Pet. 2:4–10). The church will last even beyond the time of Christ's return, and any predictions that warn of the demise of the church of Jesus Christ are greatly mistaken.

The Body of Christ

Christ is the head of the church, which is his body (Eph. 1:22–23; 4:15; 5:23). He has authority over his people and determines their direction and destiny. Each member of Christ's body serves an important and distinct role, and none have life, power, or ability of any kind apart from Christ (1 Corinthians 12).

The Bride of Christ

Christ saves and sanctifies his people through his sacrifice on the cross, which serves as the model of the relationship between a husband and wife (Eph. 5:25). Christ's self-sacrificial love for his bride continues as he feeds and cares for her—she who will one day be presented to him in spotless perfection (Eph. 5:29; Heb. 12:23). As the bride of Christ, the church should strive for undiluted devotion to Christ, who is her jealous husband (2 Cor. 11:2–4). God's people should be motivated by and longing for the great wedding banquet as they await the return of their Bridegroom (Rev. 19:7–9; 21:1–4).

The Family of God

God's adoption of lost and rebellious children into his family is a key aspect of his redeeming work (1 John 3:1–2). This adoption through new birth leads to astounding privileges that come with being fellow heirs with Christ. Those in God's family become full beneficiaries of all his promises to his children! As adopted children of God, believers are bound by a family relationship as brothers and sisters that is greater and more enduring than biological family ties (Mark 3:31–35; see Matt. 19:29). Earnest brotherly love should characterize relationships within the church (Rom. 12:10; 1 Tim. 5:1–2; Heb. 13:1; 1 Pet. 1:22). Such love is one of the primary ways Christians know they have truly been saved by God: "We know that we have passed out of death into life, because we love the brothers . . ." (1 John 3:14). All earthly obstacles to brotherly affection (e.g., differences in culture, race, income, personality, and nationality) are done away with when God adopts his people into his family (Gal. 3:28).

To love Christ means to love his church and seek to build it by word and deed. The sin and apathy often seen in the church may at times require strong criticism and be a cause for grief. But Christ shed his own blood to create the church (Acts 20:28), and the church is God's primary conduit of his grace and glory to the world. There should be no doubt that by the grace of God his community of unworthy redeemed sinners will be triumphant and beautiful one day. Meaningful local church involvement is not an optional spiritual discipline; it is the essential context within which believers are intended to find Christ and grow in him.

SCRIPTURE MEMORY AND MEDITATION

"So then you are no longer strangers and aliens, but you are fellow citizens with the saints and members of the household of God, built on the foundation of the apostles and prophets, Christ Jesus himself being the cornerstone, in whom the whole structure, being joined together, grows into a holy temple in the Lord. In him you also are being built together into a dwelling place for God by the Spirit." (Eph. 2:19–22)

Questions for Application and Discussion

1. When you look at Christians, is it difficult for you to believe that they are God's chosen people, the bride of Christ, and those who will reign with him? Why do you think God would choose such frail, often foolish people to represent him? How have you seen God's grace at work among his people?

2. Among the images of the church in this chapter, was there one that was most significant in your understanding of how God sees his people?

3. How should the image of the church as Christ's bride deepen your respect for the church and challenge your criticism of it?

4. From a biblical perspective, when do you think a church loses the right to be called a true church?

5. What has your experience with the church been like? Do you think the New Testament has any conception of a faithful Christian who is not a meaningful part of a local church?

For Further Study

Baxter, Richard. *The Reformed Pastor*. Carlisle, PA: Banner of Truth, 1979.

Clowney, Edmund. *The Doctrine of the Church*. Philadelphia: Presbyterian and Reformed, 1969.

Dever, Mark. *Nine Marks of a Healthy Church*. Wheaton, IL: Crossway, 2004.

DeYoung, Kevin, and Ted Kluck, *Why We Love the Church: In Praise of Institutions and Organized Religion*. Chicago: Moody, 2009.

Frame, John M. *Worship in Spirit and Truth*. Phillipsburg, NJ: P&R, 1996.

Keller, Timothy J. *Ministries of Mercy: The Call of the Jericho Road*. 2nd ed. Phillipsburg, NJ: Presbyterian and Reformed, 1997.

Kistler, Don, ed. *Feed My Sheep: A Passionate Plea for Preaching*. 2nd ed. Lake Mary, FL: Reformation Trust, 2008.

Moore, Russell D. *The Kingdom of Christ: The New Evangelical Perspective*. Wheaton, IL: Crossway, 2007.

Stott, John. *The Living Church: Convictions of a Lifelong Pastor*. Downers Grove, IL: InterVarsity, 2007.

Strauch, Alexander. *Biblical Eldership: An Urgent Call to Restore Biblical Church Leadership*. Littleton, CO: Lewis and Roth, 1986.

HOW WILL IT ALL END?

THE RETURN OF CHRIST

The return of Jesus Christ is the central hope of the New Testament. His second coming will be sudden (Matt. 24:44; 2 Pet. 3:10), personal, bodily (John 14:3; Acts 1:11; 1 Thess. 4:16), and visible to the whole world (Rev. 1:7). He will come again to reign in power as the King of kings for all eternity (Phil. 2:9–11). Although Scripture gives signs that will indicate that the end times are near (Matt. 24:14, 23–29; Mark 13:10, 19–26; 2 Thess. 2:1–10), God has not revealed the time of Christ's return (Matt. 24:44; Mark 13:32–33; Luke 12:40). Therefore, the setting of dates is fruitless and unbiblical speculation. The warnings that Christ will come unexpectedly and suddenly are intended to motivate believers to live in eager expectation and preparedness, which involves holy living and having an eternal perspective. Followers of Christ are to "renounce ungodliness and worldly passions, and to live self-controlled, upright, and godly lives in the present age, waiting for our blessed hope, the appearing of the glory of our great God and Savior Jesus Christ" (Titus 2:12–13). As good as life in this world may be at times, it can never compare to the ultimate liberation from sin and the unhindered fellowship with Christ that his return will bring (1 John 3:2). This does not preclude Christians from deeply investing in and appreciating this world; it only means that believers should realize that the best is yet to come and they should ultimately live for the day when Christ returns. Their greatest hope and the definitive solution to present suffering are to be found in Christ's return. On that day "the Lord himself will descend from heaven with a cry of command, with the voice of an archangel, and with the sound of the trumpet of God. And the dead in Christ will rise first. Then we who are alive, who are left, will be caught up together with them in the clouds to meet the Lord in the air, and so we will always be with the Lord" (1 Thess. 4:16–17). Christians are commanded to "encourage one another with these words" (1 Thess. 4:18), which are filled with hope.

THE MILLENNIAL REIGN OF CHRIST

Revelation speaks of Christ reigning for "a thousand years," when Satan is bound and some of God's people come to life to reign with him (Rev. 20:1–10). Christians have interpreted this millennium in one of three ways: amillennialism, premillennialism, and postmillennialism. (1) *Amillennialists* believe that the thousand years in Revelation 20 is figurative language, and that the reign of Christ from heaven is *presently* being fulfilled in the church age and will continue until the return of Christ. In this view, all the end-time events, such as Christ's return and the final judgment, happen at the same time. (2) *Premillennialists* believe that long before the final judgment, Christ will first return and establish his millennial kingdom—that is, his reign as King over all the earth for one thousand years. Within this view there are various views of the timing of the great tribulation (whether Christians will go through it or will escape it by being suddenly removed from the earth before the tribulation begins), and of whether the one thousand years is a literal or a symbolic number. (3) *Postmillennialists* believe the millennial reign of Christ will be ushered in after remarkable gospel progress establishes Christ's reign on earth, not with Christ physically present but with the majority of the world being obedient to him, and that at the end of that "millennium," Christ will return in bodily form to reign over the new heavens and new earth forever.

While there has been much debate over the nature and timing of the millennial events, what is certainly clear in Scripture is that Christ will return and establish his kingdom and that all mankind will finally acknowledge his lordship over all creation. Once and for all, creation will undeniably submit to Christ the King, and he will reign on earth as already he does in heaven (Matt. 6:10; Phil. 2:10).

THE FINAL JUDGMENT AND HELL

God expresses both personal (Rom. 1:18–32) and national judgment (Isaiah 13–23), and his judgments have taken place throughout history and in the heavenly realm (2 Pet. 2:4). But after the millennium (or, according to amillennialists, after the present age) Christ will judge the whole world once and for all (Matt. 25:31–33; 2 Tim. 4:1; Rev. 20:11–15). At this time the righteous wrath of a holy God will be unleashed on a rebellious world (Rom. 2:5; 3:19). Jesus often warned that he would usher in the day of wrath (Matt. 10:15; 11:22, 24; 12:36; 25:31–46), and other New Testament writers repeated this idea (1 Cor. 4:5; Heb. 6:2; 2 Pet. 2:4; Jude 6). Unbelievers will be judged, and the result will be punishment for even careless words that were spoken (Matt. 12:36). Those who refuse God's gracious offer of forgiveness in Christ will suffer eternal conscious punishment in hell, a condition of torment cut off from the presence of God (Matt. 25:30, 41, 46; Mark 9:43, 48; Rev. 14:9–11). Christian believers, who understand the holiness and justice of God and the depth of human sin, should be able to relate to the martyrs in heaven who long for the day of judgment (Rev. 6:10). However, in this age, the church is primarily called to warn people everywhere to repent and flee the wrath that will come when Christ returns as Judge: "The times of ignorance God overlooked, but now he commands all people everywhere to repent, because he has fixed a day on which he will judge the world in righteousness by a man whom he has appointed; and of this he has given assurance to all by raising him from the dead" (Acts 17:30–31).

Believers, as well as unbelievers, will be judged by Christ. As the apostle Paul writes to the Christians at Corinth: "We must all appear before the judgment seat of Christ, so that each one may receive what is due for what he has done in the body, whether good or evil" (2 Cor. 5:10; see Rom. 2:6–11; 14:10–12; Rev. 20:12, 15). The judgment of believers will test the worth of the way they lived. It will reveal some tragic lack of true good works in the sanctification process and will show that some were saved "but only as through fire" (1 Cor. 3:15). Here the testing ("fire") of God's judgment at the return of Christ will reveal the quality of a believer's works, and some will have little to show for their salvation. On the other hand, what was done to glorify God will be rewarded (1 Cor. 4:5; Col. 3:23–24). Although God seeks to motivate his people to holy living by the rewards they will receive, ultimately, believers can stand before God only because of Christ's finished work on their behalf. The only basis for justification is the perfect righteousness imputed to believers and the diverting of sin's penalty from them to Christ, and never the false security of self-righteousness (2 Cor. 5:21; Phil. 3:8–9). There is no fear of the final judgment for those who have trusted Christ for salvation because there is "no condemnation for those who are in Christ Jesus" (Rom. 8:1), which means they "have confidence for the day of judgment . . ." (1 John 4:17).

THE NEW HEAVENS AND NEW EARTH

God's creation of the new heavens and earth is the final phase of his redeeming work. The restored creation will be freed from the tragic effects of sin and the curse, and perfect fellowship with God will be restored. The Old Testament promised this wonderful reality as the culmination of the new covenant: "For behold, I create new heavens and a new earth, and the former things shall not be remembered or come into mind" (Isa. 65:17). The New Testament writers still long for God to finish his work in this way, as Peter says, "but according to his promise we are waiting for new heavens and a new earth in which righteousness dwells" (2 Pet. 3:13). John's Revelation gives a powerful glimpse of the end of all things: "Then I saw a new heaven and a new earth, for the first heaven and the first earth had passed away, and the sea was no more. And I saw the holy city, new Jerusalem, coming down out of heaven from God, prepared as a bride adorned for her husband" (Rev. 21:1–2). The entire world that was subjected to futility and decay in the fall will be freed from this bondage "far as the curse is found" when God recreates everything anew (Rom. 8:19–23; 2 Pet. 3:13; Rev. 21:1). There will be a joining together of heaven and the renewed earth (Rev. 21:1–3), and in company with Jesus Christ their Lord, God's people will work, play, eat, learn, and worship in their resurrected, glorified bodies (Luke 22:18; Rev. 19:9; 22:1–2). Down through the ages the church has called this place heaven, but the Bible calls it "a new heaven and a new earth" (Rev. 21:1). The very goodness of the original creation (Gen. 1:31) will here be restored and redeemed to perfection.

The knowledge of God's future restoration of all creation should deepen one's appreciation of the created order now. The created physical realm, although marred by the fall, maintains a goodness that is redeemable; God intends it to be enjoyed now as his abundant blessing: "For everything created by God is good, and nothing is to be rejected if it is received with thanksgiving, for it is made holy by the word of God and prayer" (1 Tim. 4:4–5). However, hope for the world to come motivates the believer to live ultimately for that world rather than this one. As Jesus said, "Do not lay up for yourselves treasures on earth, where moth and rust destroy and where thieves break in and steal, but lay up for yourselves treasures in heaven, where neither moth nor rust destroys and where thieves do not break in and steal. For where your treasure is, there your heart will be also" (Matt. 6:19–21). The tremendous blessing of a restored heaven and earth will be cause for extravagant praise, but the greatest blessing will be the glorious presence of God himself, and of Jesus our Lord and Savior. Fellowship with Jesus, it has been said, is what makes heaven to be heaven, and that is something that Christians will be proving true for all eternity.

SCRIPTURE MEMORY AND MEDITATION

"Behold! I tell you a mystery. We shall not all sleep, but we shall all be changed, in a moment, in the twinkling of an eye, at the last trumpet. For the trumpet will sound, and the dead will be raised imperishable, and we shall be changed." (1 Cor. 15:51–52)

Questions for Application and Discussion

1. Why do you think God's plan includes thousands of years before the return of Christ? Why do you think we may find that odd? Why do you think he has waited all this time without bringing human history to a conclusion?

2. Do you think much about Christ's second coming? Why do you think past generations of Christians

seemed to think about it far more than we do today? Why do you think the New Testament teaches about Christ's second coming as frequently as it does? If Christ came back today, do you think you will have missed out on anything life on earth offers?

3. Do you have a view on the timing of Christ's return or the millennium? Why do you think Christians in certain eras have deemed Christ's return a significant issue? What are some practical implications of the different views?

4. Do you look forward to going to heaven? What do you think it will be like? Do you ever think it will be boring? What might lead to this conclusion?

5. What habits in your life are storing up treasure in heaven? What things could be considered wood, hay, and stubble that won't survive the final judgment? What would help you live more for what lasts forever?

For Further Study

Archer, Gleason, Paul Feinberg, Douglas Moo, and Richard Reiter. *The Rapture: Pre-, Mid-, or Post-Tribulational?* Grand Rapids, MI: Zondervan, 1984.

Bavinck, Herman. *Reformed Dogmatics* Vol. 4. Grand Rapids, MI: Baker Academic, 2008.

Blamires, Harry. *Knowing the Truth about Heaven and Hell.* Knowing the Truth Series, J. I. Packer and Peter Kreeft, eds.. Ann Arbor, MI: Servant, 1988.

Clouse, Robert G., ed. *The Meaning of the Millennium: Four Views.* Downers Grove, IL: InterVarsity Press, 1977.

Dumbrell, William J. *The Search for Order: Biblical Eschatology in Focus.* Grand Rapids, MI: Baker, 1992.

Erickson, Millard. *Contemporary Options in Eschatology.* Grand Rapids, MI: Baker, 1977.

Gerstner, John H. *Repent or Perish*. Ligonier, PA: Soli Deo Gloria, 1990.

Hoekema, Anthony A. "The New Earth" in *The Bible and the Future*. Grand Rapids, MI: Eerdmans, 1979.

Kreeft, Peter. *Heaven: The Heart's Deepest Longing*. Expanded ed. San Francisco: Ignatius, 1989.

Ladd, George Eldon. *The Blessed Hope*. Grand Rapids, MI: Eerdmans, 1956.

Martin, James P. *The Last Judgment*. Grand Rapids, MI: Eerdmans, 1983.

Morgan, Christopher W., and Robert Peterson, eds. *Hell under Fire: Modern Scholarship Reinvents Eternal Punishment*. Grand Rapids, MI: Zondervan, 2004.

Smith, Wilbur M. *The Biblical Doctrine of Heaven*. Chicago: Moody, 1968.

Van Gemeren, Willem. *The Progress of Redemption*. Grand Rapids, MI: Zondervan, 1988.

Walvoord, John F. *The Blessed Hope and the Tribulation*. Grand Rapids, MI: Zondervan, 1976.

CONCLUSION

As we have sought to understand the answers God gives in the Bible to life's biggest questions, I hope you have not missed the main point in the midst of all that's been said. The entire message of the Bible can be summarized in this one sentence: The one true God is displaying his glory primarily in redeeming and restoring his fallen creation by fulfilling his covenant promises and commands through the glorious person and atoning work of Christ. Or even more simply, God made us for his glory, we reject him as our King, Jesus saves us. The Bible itself puts it this way: "For all have sinned and fall short of the glory of God, and are justified by his grace as a gift, through the redemption that is in Christ Jesus, whom God put forward as a propitiation [a sacrifice that satisfies God's wrath] by his blood, to be received by faith . . ." (Rom. 3:23–25).

We've been asking God a lot of questions. The main question he asks of you is, will you trust his gracious gift of forgiveness in Christ, or will you insist on paying the penalty yourself? No one has the ability to earn God's favor; it all depends on responding to his astonishing offer of grace in Christ with repentance and faith. God loves to forgive and save rebels from sin and death. That is the answer we all need most.

SCRIPTURE MEMORY AND MEDITATION

"Because, if you confess with your mouth that Jesus is Lord and believe in your heart that God raised him from the dead, you will be saved. (Rom. 10:9)

Questions for Application and Discussion

1. What do you think the main message of the Bible is?
2. How would you define the gospel or explain the main reason Jesus came?
3. Do you believe you need forgiveness? If so, what would it take for you to be forgiven by God?
4. Do you believe that Jesus is both God and man and is the only way to a restored relationship with God? What do you think Jesus meant when he said, "I am the way and the truth and the life. No one comes to the Father except through me" (John 14:6)?
5. Have you ever trusted Christ for the forgiveness of your sins? If not, what is preventing you from doing that today?

For Further Study

2 Ways to Live: The Choice We All Face. Matthias Media, 2003. http://www.matthiasmedia.com.au/2wtl/.

Carson, D. A. *The God Who Is There: Finding Your Place in God's Story.* Grand Rapids, MI: Baker, 2010.

Piper, John. *God Is the Gospel: Meditations of God's Love as the Gift of Himself.* Wheaton: Crossway, 2005.

SCRIPTURE INDEX

175